US Army Operator's & Maintenance Manuals for the M1911A1 Caliber .45 Semiautomatic Pistol:

Consisting of TM 9-1005-211-12 Operator's Manual & TM 9-1005-211-35 Direct Support Maintenance Manual

US Army

Battles & Book Reviews Publishing

ISBN: **1535551798**

ISBN-13: **978-1535551793**

TABLE OF CONTENTS

iv

EDITOR'S NOTE

This volume contains two US Army Manuals:

- Technical Manual 9-1005-211-12 – The Operator and Organizational maintenance manual for the M1911A1
- Technical Manual 9-1005-211-35 – The Direct Support, General Support, & Depot level maintenance manual for the M1911A1

Both are manuals that are difficult to find in print and when you do, they are almost prohibitively expensive. I put this volume together because I personally own and love the M1911 .45 ACP pistol. I think there is no better pistol ever manufactured for personal defense and John Browning's design has proved that by more than withstanding the test of time.

Think about the history of the pistol. It was first designed in 1902 and accepted into US government service in 1911 and remained the US Military's standard sidearm for the next 74 years until it was replaced by the M9, 9mm pistol from Beretta. Ironically, the Beretta proved itself a combat failure in Iraq and Afghanistan and the US Army is searching for a replacement as of 2014, with the M1911 being on the short list for reintroduction.

I picked these manuals because I find them the most useful of the Army manuals, which are written such that just about anybody can easily understand them. It is an oft repeated saw in the Army that all manuals are written at an eighth grade level. I am not sure that is true but I am certain that these two manuals are written in clear, unambiguous language that is easy to understand. I have included the wealth of images from the original manuals

The TM's are the maintenance manuals and they detail proven methods of inspection, cleaning, and repair. They include detailed assembly and disassembly instructions and are richly illustrated. Since as civilians we cannot just turn our weapons into the armorer for repair. Our choices are either fix a broken weapon ourselves or pay a gunsmith. The beauty of the 1911 is that many repairs are easily done by a non-professional and these manuals show you how to do it.

I also find that the list of repair parts is instructive and provides a good guide for what parts a 1911 owner should have on hand as part of their preparation kit.

I have omitted the Stock number indexes from the TM's and redone most of the tables so that are more easily read the poor scans I had while consulting my original copies of these manuals.

My goal in compiling and editing these was to make them available at an affordable price using modern Print-On-Demand (POD) technology. I hope these manuals are instructive and useful to owners of a 1911 or clone who did not have the benefit of detailed maintenance and repair manuals before.

TM 9-1005-211-12

Technical Manual
No. 9-1005-211-12

HEADQUARTERS,
DEPARTMENT OF THE ARMY
Washington, D.C., 18 September 1988

OPERATOR AND ORGANIZATIONAL MAINTENANCE MANUAL INCLUDING BASIC ISSUE ITEMS LIST AND REPAIR PARTS AND SPECIAL TOOLS LIST

PISTOL, CALIBER .45, AUTOMATIC, M1911A1 # WITH HOLSTER, HIP (1005-673-7965) AND PISTOL, CALIBER .45, AUTOMATIC, M1911 A1, WITH HOLSTER, SHOULDER (1005-561-2003)

INCORPORATING CHANGES 1-4
This manual is current as of 18 September 1988.

CHAPTER 1 INTRODUCTION

SECTION I. GENERAL

1-1. Scope

This manual contains instructions for the operator and organizational maintenance personnel of the Caliber .46 Automatic Pistol M1911A1 as allocated by the Maintenance Allocation Chart

1-2. Forms and Records

    a.   General. DA Forms and procedures used for equipment maintenance will be only those prescribed in TM 88-760, Army Equipment Record Procedures.

    b.   Recommendations for Equipment Publication Improvements. Report of errors, omissions, and recommendations for improving this publication by the individual user is encouraged. Reports should be submitted on DA Form 2028 (Recommended Changes to DA Publications) and forwarded direct to the Commanding General, U.S. Army Weapons Command, ATTN: AMSWB-SMM-P, Rock Island, Illinois 61201.

SECTION II. DESCRIPTION AND DATA

1-3. General

The Caliber .45 Automatic Pistol M1911A1 (figs 1-1 and 1-2) is a recoil operated hand weapon. It is fed from a seven round magazine and is a semiautomatic weapon, firing one round each time the trigger is squeezed. The weapon can be carried in either a hip or shoulder holster. The pistol can be broken down into two major groups (fig. 1-3).

Figure 1-1: Caliber .45 Automatic Pistol, M1911A1 - right front view

Figure 1-2: Caliber .45 Automatic Pistol, M1911A1 - left rear view

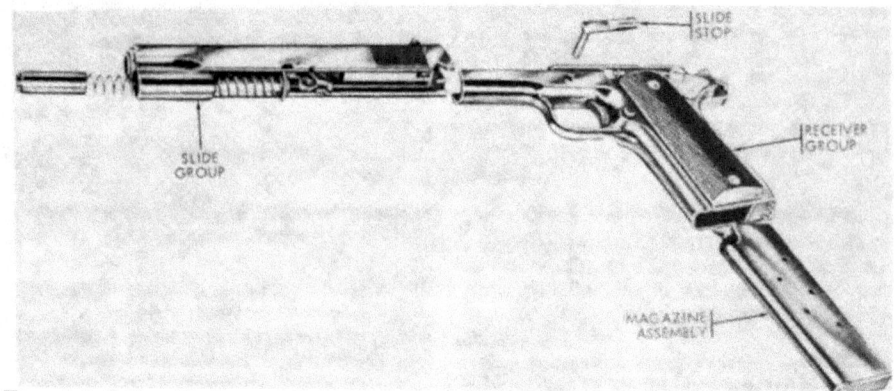

Figure 1-3: Caliber .45 Automatic Pistol, M1911A1 - major groups and assemblies

1-4. Tabulated Data

Length	8-5/8 in
Weight:	
Empty magazine	2.6 lb. (approx.)
Loaded magazine	3.0 lb. (approx.)
Height of front sight above axis of bore	0.5597 in
Sight radius	6.481 in
Muzzle velocity (max)	830 fps
Maximum range	1500m
Maximum effective range	50m
Trigger pull	6 to 6-1/2 lb.
Diameter of bore (caliber)	0.45 in
Number of lands and grooves	6
Rifling, left hand	one turn in 16 in.
Length of barrel	5.03 in
Length of rifling	4.118 in. (min)
Depth of grooves	0.003 in.
Cooling system	air

CHAPTER 2 OPERATING INSTRUCTIONS

SECTION I. SERVICE UPON RECEIPT OF MATERIEL

2-1. General

Refer to table 2-1.

Table 2-1 - Service upon Receipt of Materiel		
Step	**Action**	**Reference**
1	Remove pistol and items from container	
2	Remove VCI packaging	
3	Check for missing items. *Note: items must agree with Basic Issue Items List (BIIL)*	App. B
4	Field strip weapon and inspect for: *Missing parts and Proper assembly*	Para. 3-9
5	Clean and Lubricate (if necessary)	Para. 3-3, 3-4, & 3-10a
6	Assemble	Para. 3-9
7	Hand function	

SECTION II. OPERATION UNDER USUAL CONDITIONS

2-2. General

Care and cleaning of the pistol includes daily preventive maintenance, which is the ordinary care of the pistol required to preserve its condition and appearance when no firing is done. Before-firing cleaning insures that the pistol is safe to fire and is properly lubricated for efficient operation, and after-firing maintenance insures that all corrosion-inducing agents are completely removed. For cleaning procedures refer to paragraph 8-lOa. For lubrication procedures refer to paragraphs 8-8 and 8-4. The operator must be thoroughly familiar with all safety features of the pistol. For safety tests, refer to table 3-2.

2-3. Loading, Firing, and Unloading

a. Loading.
Warning. *Care must be exercised to either have the pistol raised or pointed down range when loading.*

Warning. *The firer must be sure that the bore of the pistol la free from any foreign matter. Firing a pistol with any obstruction in the bore win result in damage to the weapon and possible Injury to personnel.*

Draw pistol from holster, insert magazine, pull slide to the rear and release, putting a round in the chamber, press the safety lock (small arms safety) up into the SAFE position.

6. Firing.

To fire the pistol, press the safety lock (small arms safety) down to the FIRE position to prevent disturbing the firing grip of the right hand. Obtain the correct sight alignment and sight picture and squeeze the trigger. To fire successive shots, the trigger must be released and squeezed again. When the last cartridge from the magazine has been fired, the slide remains to the rear.

e. Unloading. To unload press the magazine catch and remove the magazine. If the slide is in the forward position, pull the slide to the rear and push the slide stop up. Inspect the chamber to ensure that the pistol is dear. Press the slide stop down, allowing the slide to go forward. Pull trigger while weapon is in safe position.

2-4. Firing Malfunctions and Stoppages

a. Malfunctions. A malfunction Is a failure of the weapon to function properly. Malfunctions are classified as defects in the weapon that normally do not cause a break in the cycle of operation.

6. Stoppages. A stoppage Is an unintentional interruption in the cycle of operation. A stoppage occurs when the pistol does not fire through no fault of the firer.

c. Immediate Action in Case of Firing Malfunctions.

(1) Immediate action is the prompt action taken by the firer to reduce a stoppage. The procedure for applying immediate action should become instinctive to the operator of the pistol. If a stoppage occurs, immediate action is applied automatically in an effort to reduce the stoppage without attempting to discover the cause at that time.

(2) In the event the slide is fully forward, the hammer falls, and the pistol fails to fire, apply immediate action as follows:

(a) Manually cock the hammer without opening the chamber and make one additional attempt to fire. If the pistol still fails to fire, wait 10 seconds, and then raise the pistol. Grasp the slide with the thumb and first finger of the non-firing hand, keeping the thumb on the right side of the slide. Pull the slide rear- ward rapidly, to its full extent. Rotate the pistol to the right allowing the unfired round to drop out, release the slide and allow it to return to the forward position, chambering a new cartridge.

Caution. *Keep the weapon pointed down range during this operation.*

(b) Aim and attempt to fire.

(3) In the event the slide is not fully forward, remove the trigger finger from the trigger guard and with the non-firing hand attempt to push the slide fully forward. If the slide will not move forward, proceed as follows:

(a) Bring the weapon to a safe position.

(b) Remove the magazine.

7

(c) Grasp the slide with the left hand, pull the slide to the rear, and lock it with the slide stop.

(d) Inspect the chamber. Remove any obstructions.

(e) Insert another loaded magazine into the pistol

(f) Release the slide.

(g) Aim and attempt to fire.

(4) If the weapon does not fire after the application of immediate action as outlined above, a detailed inspection should be made to determine the cause of the stoppage.

SECTION III. OPERATION UNDER UNUSUAL CONDITIONS

2-5. General

In addition to the normal operation of the pistol, special care in cleaning and lubrication must be observed where extremes of temperature, humidity, and atmospheric conditions exist or are anticipated. Proper cleaning, lubrication, storage, and handling of lubricants not only Ensure operation of the weapon, but also guard against wear of the working parts and deterioration of the material.

2-6. Operation in Extreme Cold

a. In temperatures below freezing, it is necessary that the moving parts of the weapon be kept free from moisture. Excess oil on working parts will solidify and cause sluggish operation or complete failure.

b. Before cleaning, allow the weapon to attain room temperature. Perform detailed disassembly (par 3-9) and complete cleaning (par 3- 10a) before use in temperatures below 0°F. Working surfaces that show signs of wear may be lubricated by rubbing lightly with a rag that has been wet with weapons lubricating oil (LAW).

2-7. Operation in Extreme Heat

a. In tropical climates where temperature and humidity are high, or where salt air is present, and during rainy seasons the weapon should be disassembled, inspected, all parts wiped dry, and lightly oiled daily.

b. In hot, dry climates where sand and dust may get into the weapon, daily disassembly, inspection and cleaning should be accomplished. After cleaning, the pistol should be wiped dry and no lubricants applied.

CHAPTER 3 OPERATOR AND ORGANIZATIONAL MAINTENANCE INSTRUCTIONS

SECTION I. OPERATORS TOOLS AND EQUIPMINT

3-1. General

For operator's tools and equipment, refer to appendix B.

SECTION II. ORGANIZATIONAL MAINTENANCE REPAIR PARTS

3-2. General

For the listing of organizational maintenance authorized repair parts refer to appendix B.

SECTION III. LUBRICATION INSTRUCTIONS

3-3. General Lubrication Instructions

a. Use lubricating oil, general purpose (PL special) for lubrication above 0°F, and weapons lubricating oil (LAW) for lubrication below 0°F on all parts of the weapon. Prior to firing all interior parts must have a light coat of oil, except the bore which must be wiped dry of any lubrication, and other interior parts that come into contact with ammunition.

b. Refer to table 3-1 for listing of lubrication and cleaning materials and stock numbers for requisitioning purposes.

Table 3-1 Lubrication and Cleaning Materials	
Federal Stock Number (FSN)	**Description**
6350-224-6656	Cleaning Compound, Rifle Bore (2 oz. Can)
6350-224-6657	Cleaning Compound, Rifle Bore (6 oz. Can)
6350-231-1985	Dry Cleaning Solvent (1 gal can)
6350-965-2332	Carbon Removing Compound (5-gal pail)

7920-205-1711	Rag, Wiping (50lb bale)
9150-273-2339	Lubricating Oil, General Purpose (PL Special) (4 oz. can)
9150-292-9689	Lubricating Oils, Weapons (LAW) (1 qt. can)

3-4. Specific Lubrication Instructions

The following areas must be well lubricated prior to firing the weapon:
- Guide rails of the receiver
- Grooves on the slide

Caution. Prior to loading the weapon, attention should be directed to wiping all visible oil from the pistol grip areas. Excessive ell could cause loco of control during firing.

SECTION IV. PREVENTIVE MAINTENANCE CHECKS AND SERVICES

3-5 Preventative Maintenance Performed by the Operator

a. The pistol should be inspected (par 8-10b) each day and cleaned (par 8-10a), if necessary.

6. Refer to table 3-2 for specific preventive maintenance checks and services to be performed by the operator.

Table 3-2 Preventive Maintenance Checks and Services

Item to be Inspected	Procedure	Reference
Pistol and Holster	General appearance and proper functioning of component parts *Warning. Before starting an inspection be sure to clear the weapon. Do not actuate the trigger until the weapon has been cleared. Remove magazine, inspect the chamber to insure that it is empty and check to see that no ammunition is in position to be introduced.*	
Safety Tests	*Safety Lock Test. With the pistol unloaded cock the hammer and Fig 8-1 press the safety upward into the safe (locked) position. Grasp the grip so the grip safety is depressed and squeeze the trigger tightly 8 or 4 times. If the hammer falls, return pistol to organizational maintenance.*	Fig. 3-1
Safety Tests	*Grip Safety Test. With the pistol unloaded, cock the hammer, and Fig 3-2 without depressing the grip safety, point the pistol downward and squeeze the trigger 8 or 4 times. If the hammer falls because the grip safety is depressed by its own weight return the pistol to organizational maintenance.*	Fig. 3-2 & 2-3
Safety Tests	*Half-Cock Position Test. With the pistol unloaded, draw back the Fig 3-8 and 14 hammer until the sear engages the half-cock position notch, then squeeze the trigger. If the hammer falls, return the pistol to organizational maintenance. Draw the hammer back nearly to full cock position, do not squeeze trigger, and then let thumb slip off hammer. The hammer should fall only to the half-cock notch.*	Fig. 3-3 & 3-4
Safety Tests	Disconnector Test. Fig 8-6 1. With the pistol unloaded, cock the hammer, push the slide group 1/4 inch to the rear and hold in that position while squeezing trigger. Let slide group go forward, maintaining pressure on trigger. If the hammer falls, return pistol to organizational maintenance. 2. Pull the slide group rearward until slide stop is engaged. Squeeze trigger and release slide group simultaneously. The hammer should not fall, if it does, return pistol to organizational maintenance. 3. Release the pressure on the trigger and then squeeze it The hammer should then fall, if it does not fall return pistol to organizational maintenance. Also, check for a faulty disconnector which would prevent the hammer from falling. The disconnector should prevent the release of the hammer unless the slide group is in a forward position and locked into battery. *Note. This also prevents the firing of more than one shot with each squeeze of the t+B9+B6:B+B5:B12*	Fig. 3-5

11

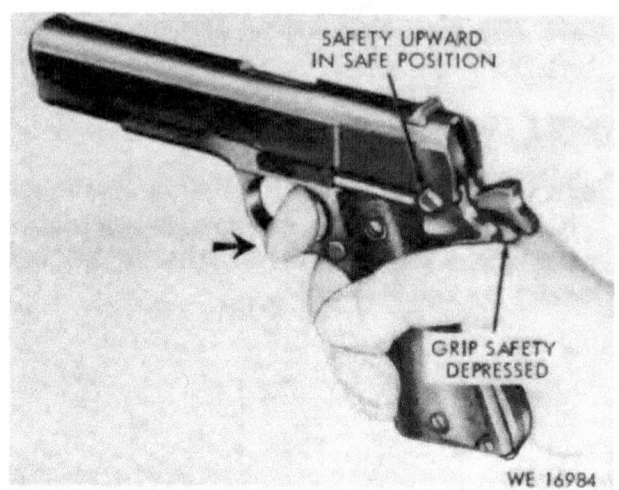

Figure 3-1. Safety Lock Test

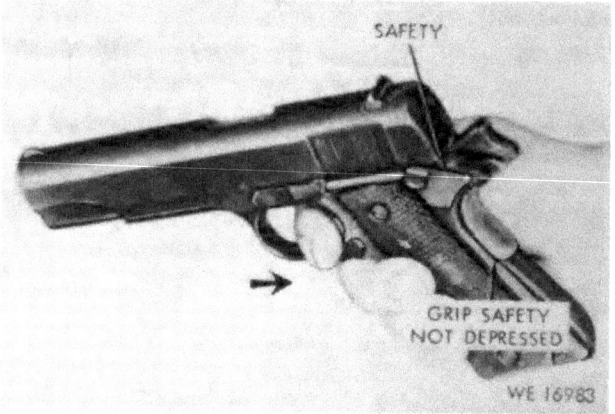

Figure 3-2. Grip Safety Test

12

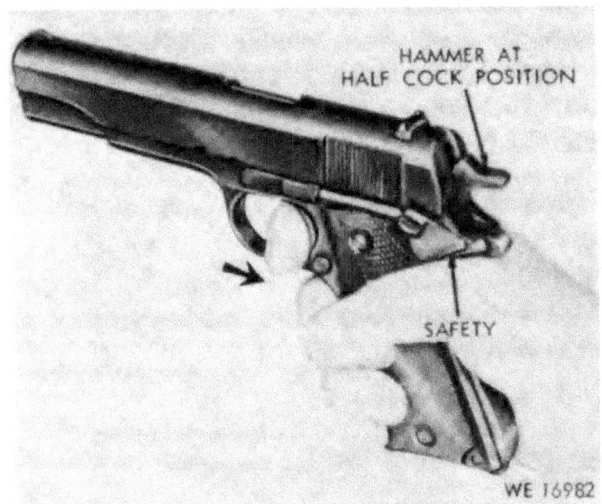

Figure 3-3. Half-Cock Position Test (1 of 2)

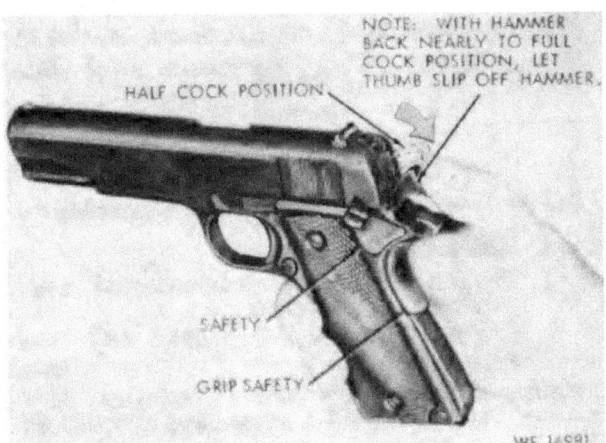

Figure 3-4. Half-cock Position Test (2 of 2)

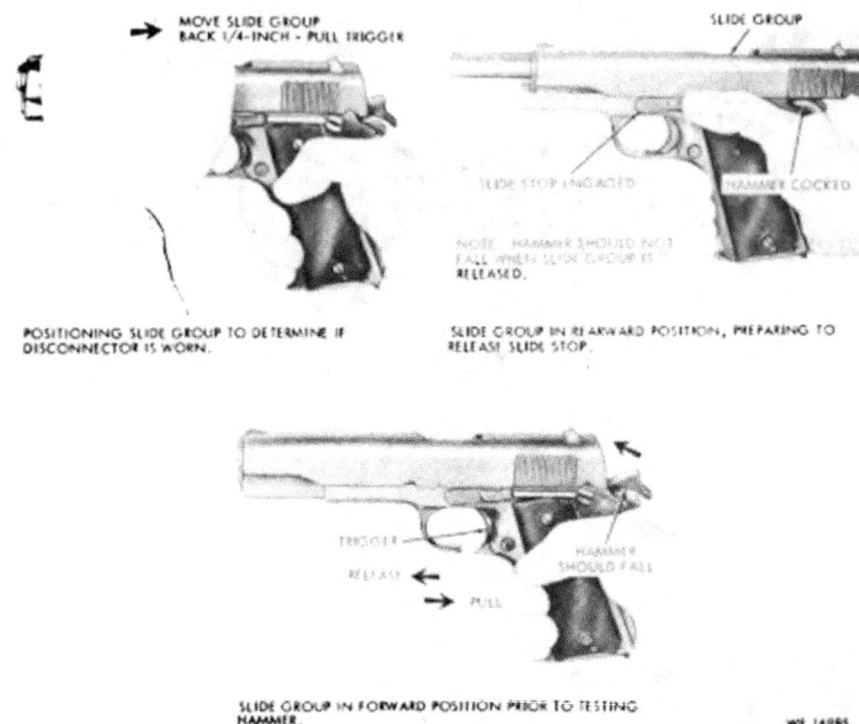

WE 16985

Figure 3-5. Disconnector Test

3-6. Preventive Maintenance Performed by Organizational Maintenance Personnel

For preventive maintenance checks and services to be performed by organizational maintenance personnel refer to table 3-2. should be performed weekly. During periods of inactivity perform preventive maintenance, every 90 days, unless inspection reveals more frequent servicing is necessary.

SECTION V. TROUBLESHOOTING

3-7. Troubleshooting by the Operator

a. Refer to table 3-3.

b. Return pistol to organizational maintenance for corrective action not authorized to the operator.

14

Table 3-3 Troubleshooting by the Operator

Malfunction	Probable Cause	Corrective Action
Failure to Feed	The Top Cartridge in the Magazine is not properly positioned	Reload Magazine
	Dirty or Rusty Magazines	Clean and Lubricate
	Improper Assembly of Magazine	Reassemble, fig. 3-9
	Broken, Damaged, or bent parts	Replace Magazine Assy. Fig. B-1
Failure to Chamber	Obstruction or Dirty Chamber	Clean Chamber
	Weak Recoil Spring	Para. 3-7b
Failure to Lock	**The barrel locking ribs do not interlock with the locking recesses in the slide.**	
	Lack of lubrication of Operating Parts	Lubricate, par 3-3 and 3-4.
	Dirty or burred barrel locking ribs or locking recesses.	Clean, Para. 3-7b
	Weak Recoil Spring	Para. 3-7b
	Broken barrel link	Para. 3-7b
Failure to Fire	**The hammer falls but the primer of the cartridge is not ignited**	
	Bent or broken hammer strut	Para. 3-7b
	Broken firing pin	Para. 3-7b
	Broken barrel lugs	Para. 3-7b
Failure to Unlock	**The barrel locking ribs do not disengage from the recesses in the slide**	
	Broken barrel link	Para. 3-7b
	Broken link pin	Para. 3-7b
	Broken barrel lugs	Para. 3-7b
Failure to Extract	**The cartridge case is not removed from the chamber.**	

	Dirty chamber.	Clean chamber, Para. 3-7b
	Pitted Chamber	Para. 3-7b
	Broken or worn extractor	Para. 3-7b
Failure to Eject	**The cartridge case is not ejected from the pistol**	
	Faulty extractor or ejector	Para. 3-7b
Failure to Cock	Defective Sear Spring	Para. 3-7b
	Worn or broken disconnector, sear or full cock notch on hammer	Para. 3-7b
Miscellaneous	Two or more shots fired in succession by one trigger squeeze	Para. 3-7b

3-8. Organizational Troubleshooting

Refer to table 3-4

Table 3-4 Organizational Troubleshooting

Malfunction	Probable Cause	Corrective Action
Failure to Chamber	Weak Recoil Spring	Para. 3-12c (3)
Failure to Lock	Dirty or burred barrel locking ribs or locking recesses.	Stone burs, Clean, Para. 3-12 & 3-12c
	Weak Recoil Spring	Para. 3-12c (3)
	Broken barrel link	Replace, 9, fig. B-1
Failure to Fire	Bent or broken hammer strut	Replace, 22, fig. B-1
Failure to Fire	Broken firing pin	Replace, 11, fig. B-1
	Broken barrel lugs	Para. 3-7b
	Weak Mainspring	Para. 3-12c (3)
Failure to Unlock	Broken barrel link	Replace, 9, fig. B-1
	Broken link pin	Replace, 3, fig. B-1

	Broken barrel lugs	Para. 3-12c (3)
Failure to Extract	Pitted Chamber	Para. 3-12c (3)
	Broken or worn extractor	Para. 3-12c (3)
Failure to Eject	Faulty extractor or ejector	Para. 3-12c (3)
Failure to Cock	Defective Sear Spring	Replace, 18, fig B-1
Failure to Cock	Worn or broken disconnector, sear or full cock notch on hammer	Para. 3-12c (3)

SECTION VI. OPERATORS MAINTENANCE PROCEDURES

3-9 Disassembly/Assembly Procedures

 a. For disassembly/assembly of the weapon authorized to the operator refer to figures 3-6 through 3-8.

 Note: *White arrows, shown on illustrations, indicate removal or disassembly sequence, arrows assembly or installation sequence.*

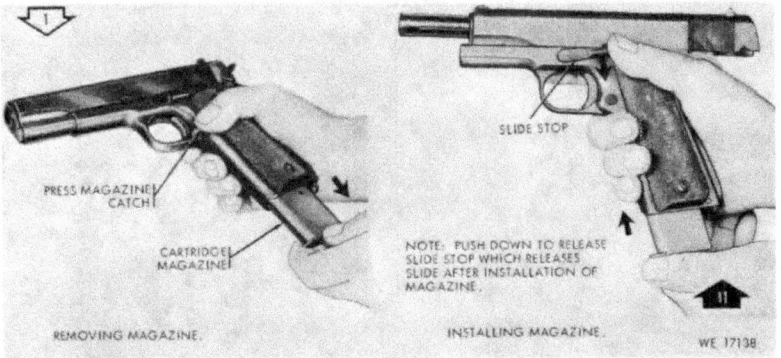

Figure 3-6. Operator's disassembly/assembly of Caliber .45 Automatic pistol, M1911A1 (1 of 3)

17

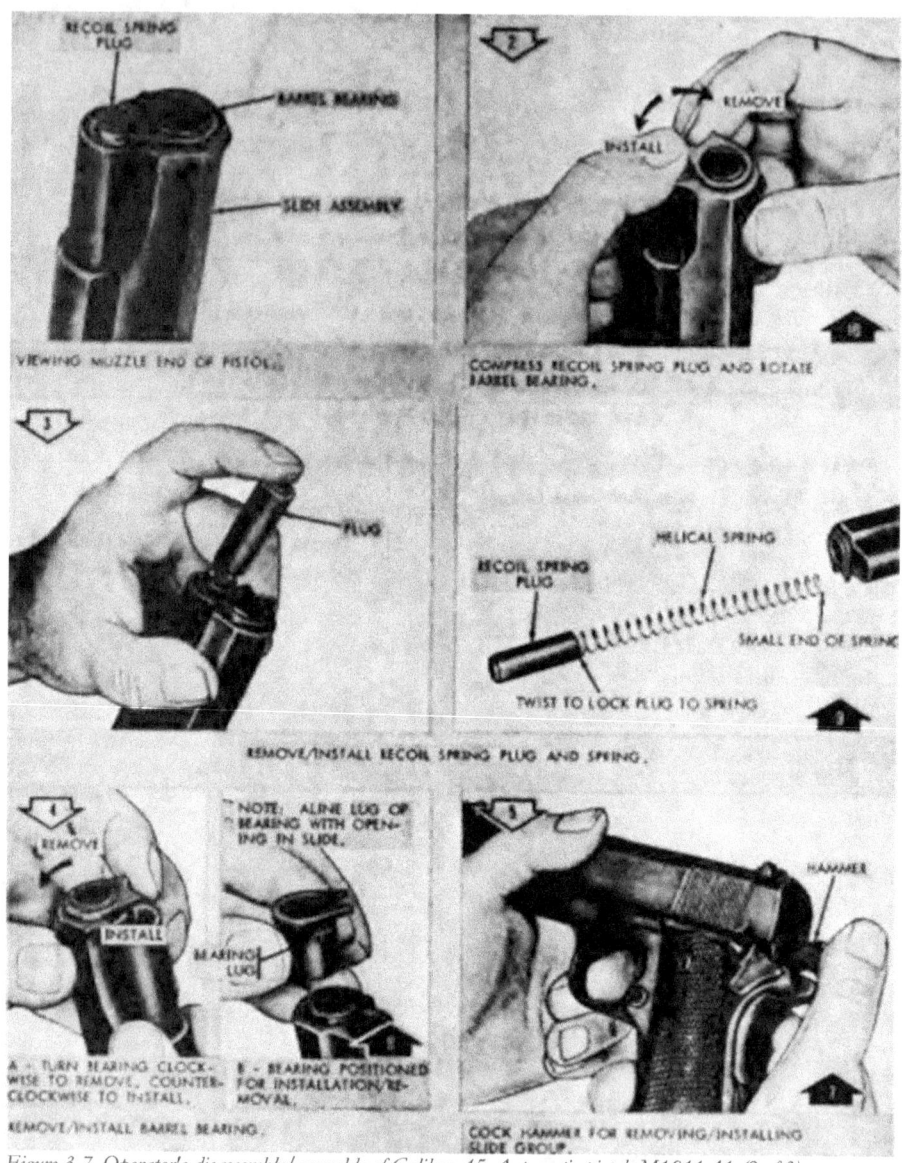

Figure 3-7. Operator's disassembly/assembly of Caliber .45 Automatic pistol, M1911A1 (2 of 3)

18

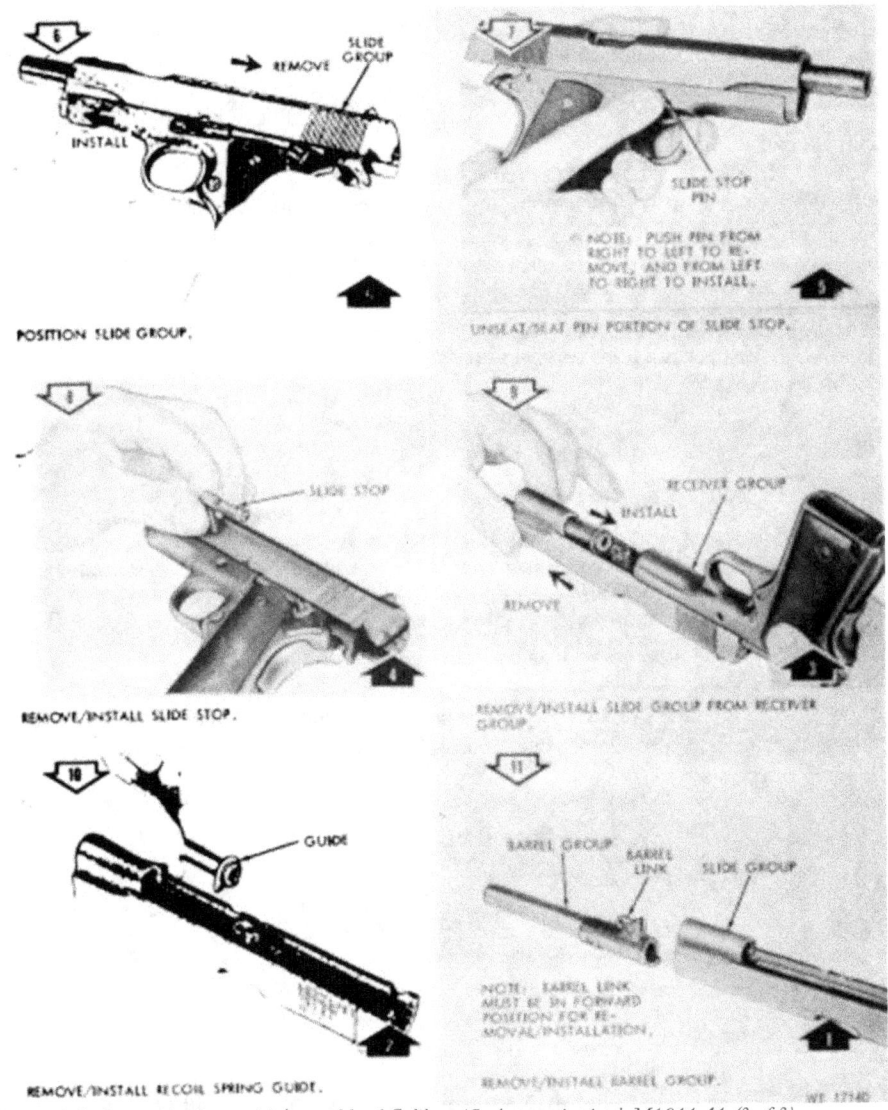

Figure 3-8. Operator's disassembly/assembly of Caliber .45 Automatic pistol, M1911A1 (3 of 3)

b. To test the pistol, for correct assembly, pull the slide fully to the rear, and release it, the hammer should remain cocked. The hammer should fall.

3-10. Cleaning, Inspection and Repair

a. Cleaning.

(1) General. Disassemble the pistol and clean all parts with a rag saturated with Rifle Bore Cleaner (RBC). Dry parts, apply a light coat of general purpose lubricating oil (PL special) and assemble the pistol.

(2) Cleaning after firing. The pistol must be thoroughly cleaned as soon as possible, after firing, in the following manner.

(a) Disassemble the pistol.

(b) Clean all parts with Rifle Bore Cleaner (RBC), dry all parts and apply a light coat of oil (PL special).

(c) Clean the bore and chamber as follows:

1. Wet a swab with Rifle Bore Cleaner (RBC) and run it back and forth through the bore several times.

2. Attach the pistol bore brush (1, fig B-2) to the cleaning rod (2, fig B-2) and run it through the bore and chamber several times.

3. Run dry swabs through the bore and chamber until they are dean.

4. Inspect the bore for cleanliness. If it is not free of all residue, repeat the cleaning process.

5. When the chamber and bore are clean, coat them lightly with oil (PL special).

6. Assemble the pistol.

7. Perform the test for correct assembly (par 3-9b).

8. Apply a light coat of oil to the exterior surfaces of the pistol.

b. Inspection. The operator should daily inspect the weapon. Particular attention should be directed to making sure the pistol is free from rust, any foreign matter, and that it is dean. Refer to table 3-2 for detailed procedures that are applicable to inspections as well as preventive maintenance.

c. Repair.

(1) Operator's repairs to the weapon will be limited to replacement of the magazine. The magazine can be disassembled in accordance with figure 8-9 for cleaning purposes.

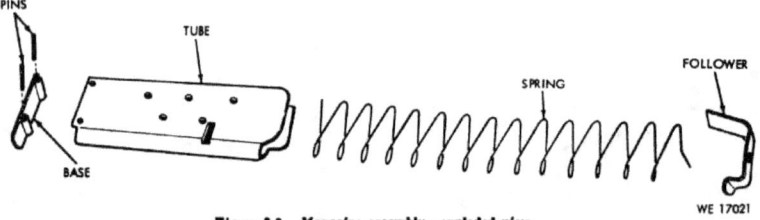

Figure 8-9. Magazine assembly—exploded view.

Figure 3-9 Magazine assembly - exploded view

(2) For repairs Other than authorized above, return pistol to organizational Maintenance personnel.

Note: *Magazine assembly (old manufacture) shown new manufactured, magazine assembly has welded base.*

SECTION VII. ORGANIZATIONAL MAINTENANCE PROCEDURES

3-11. Disassembly/ Assembly Procedures

Refer to figures 3-10 through 3-15 for detailed procedures on disassembly/assembly of the pistol.

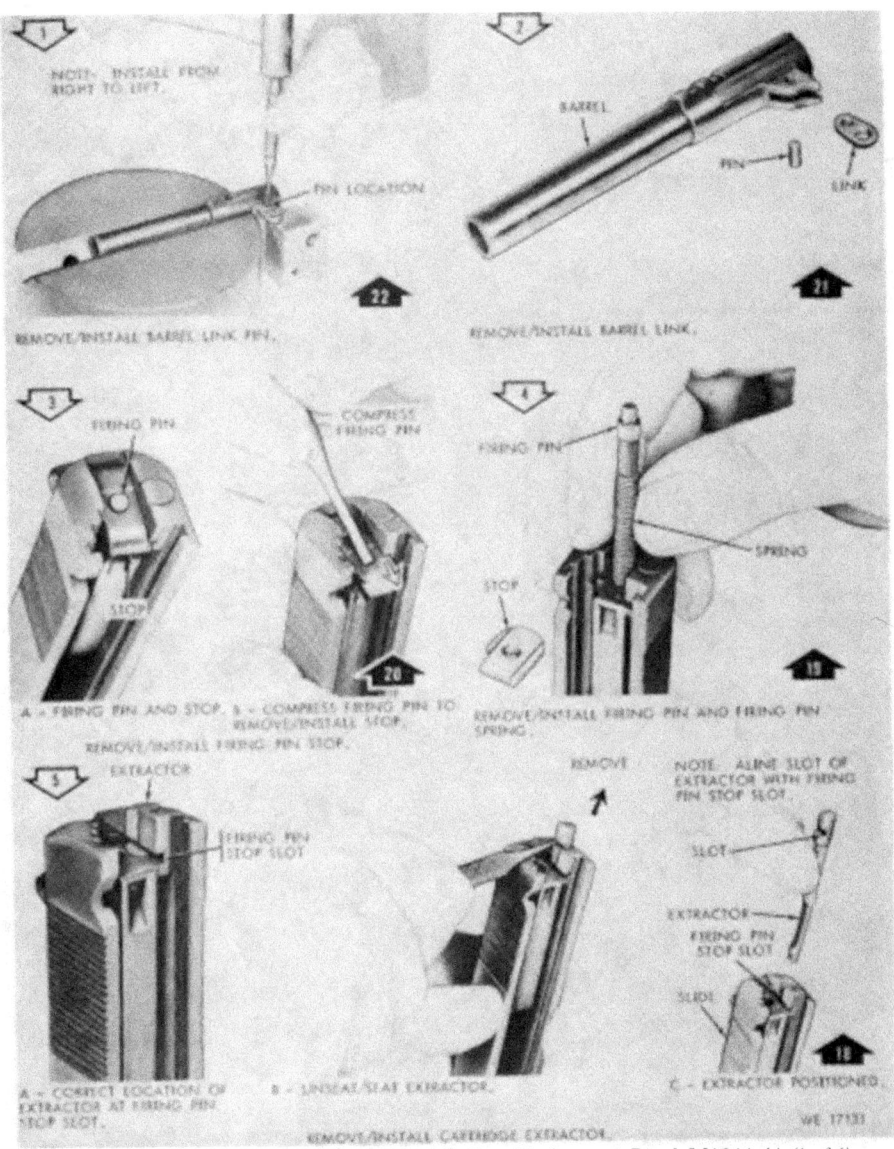

Figure 3-10 Organizational disassembly/assembly of Caliber .45 Automatic Pistol, M1911A1 (1 of 6)

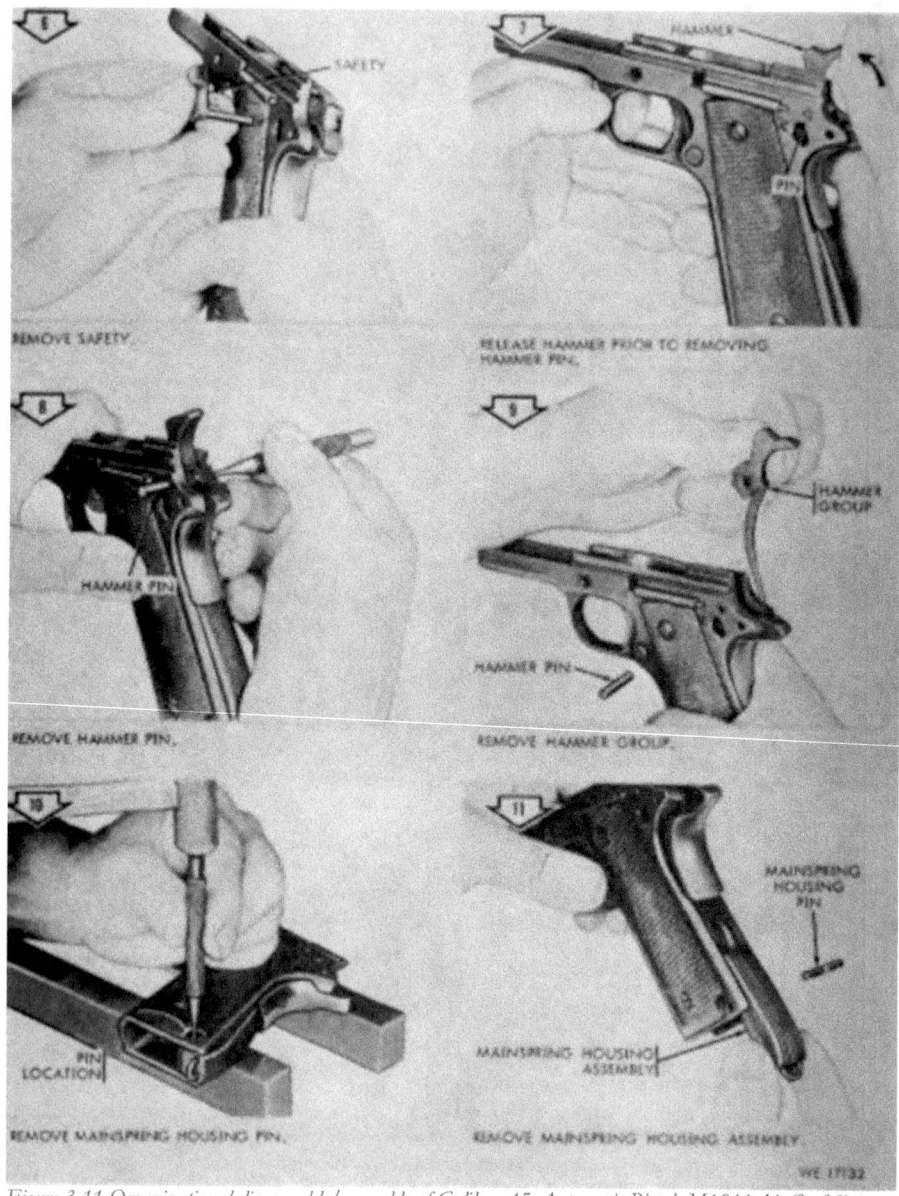

Figure 3-11 Organizational disassembly/assembly of Caliber .45 Automatic Pistol, M1911A1 (2 of 6)

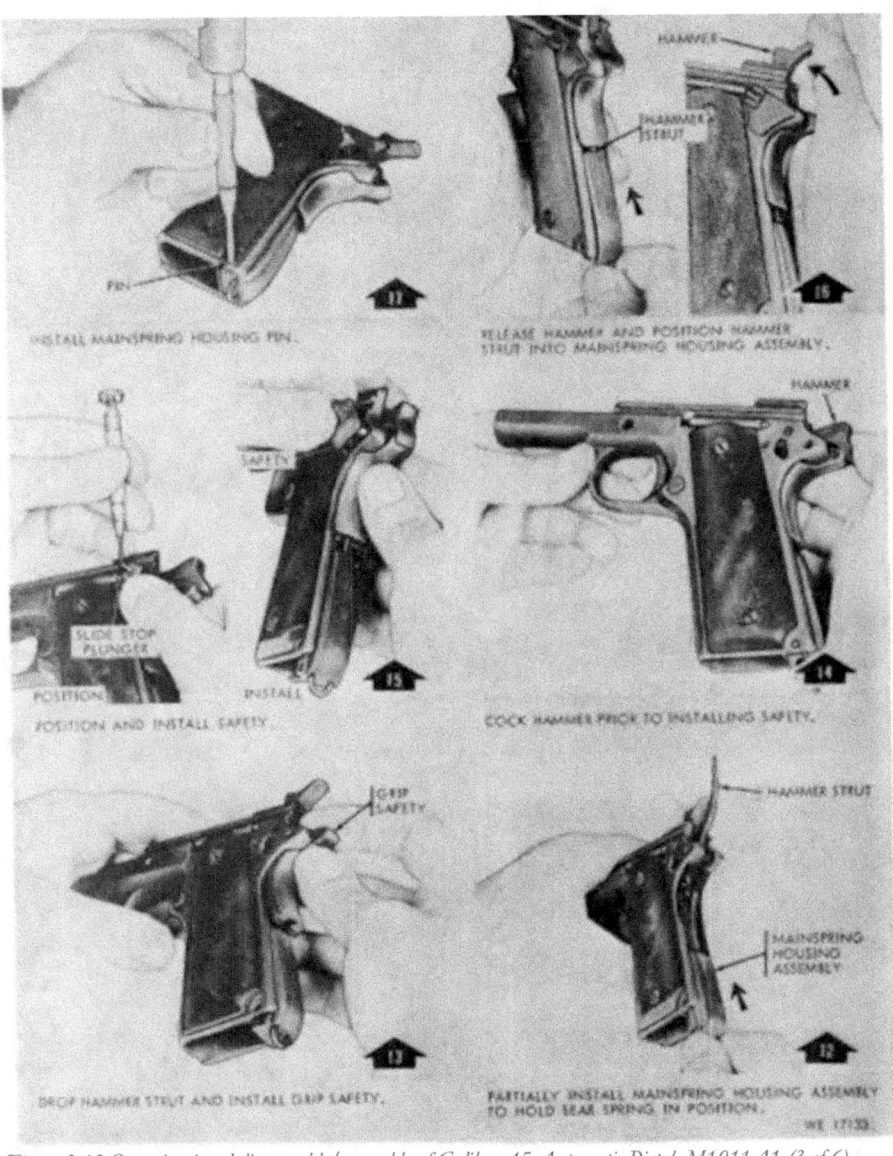

INSTALL MAINSPRING HOUSING PIN.

RELEASE HAMMER AND POSITION HAMMER STRUT INTO MAINSPRING HOUSING ASSEMBLY.

HAMMER

HAMMER STRUT

POSITION AND INSTALL SAFETY.

COCK HAMMER PRIOR TO INSTALLING SAFETY.

HAMMER

SLIDE STOP PLUNGER

SAFETY

POSITION

INSTALL

GRIP SAFETY

HAMMER STRUT

MAINSPRING HOUSING ASSEMBLY

DROP HAMMER STRUT AND INSTALL GRIP SAFETY.

PARTIALLY INSTALL MAINSPRING HOUSING ASSEMBLY TO HOLD SEAR SPRING IN POSITION.

WE 17133

Figure 3-12 Organizational disassembly/assembly of Caliber .45 Automatic Pistol, M1911A1 (3 of 6)

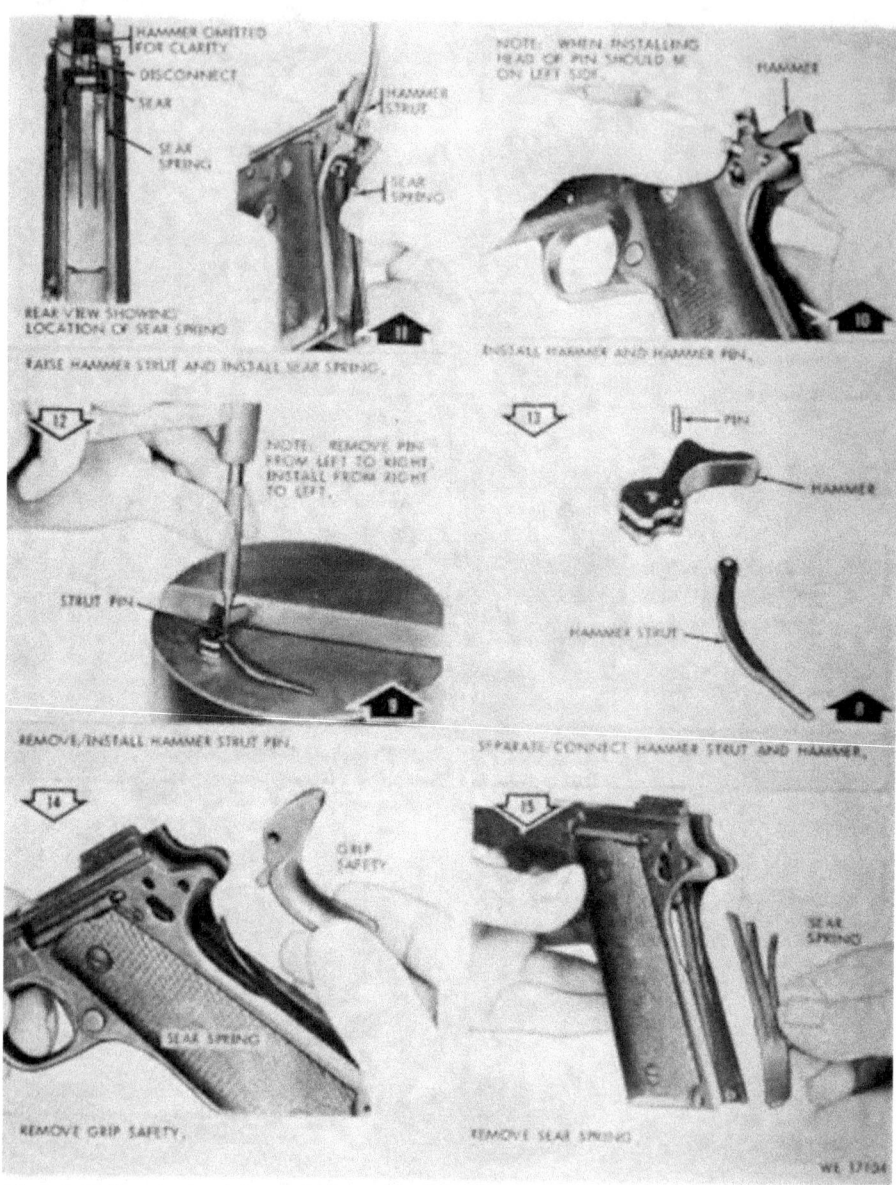

Figure 3-13 Organizational disassembly/assembly of Caliber .45 Automatic Pistol, M1911A1 (3 of 6)

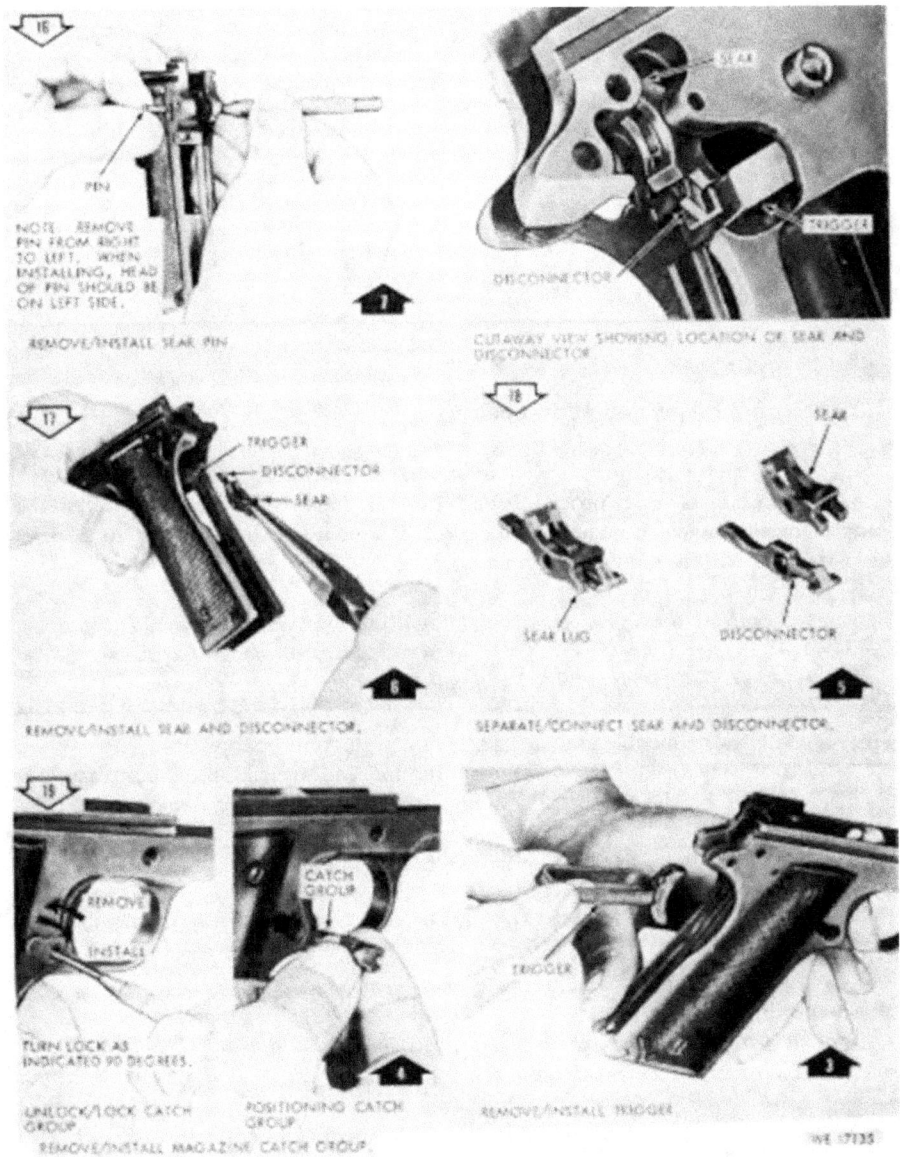

Figure 3-14 Organizational disassembly/assembly of Caliber .45 Automatic Pistol, M1911A1 (5 of 6)

25

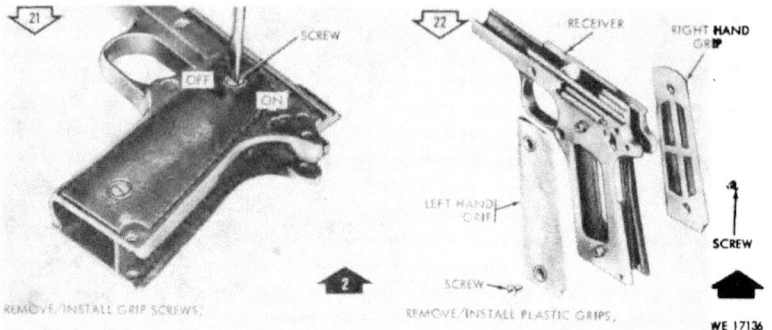

Figure 3-15 Organizational disassembly/assembly of Caliber .45 Automatic Pistol, M1911A1 (6 of 6)

3-12. Cleaning, Inspection and Repair

a. Cleaning. For general cleaning instructions refer to TM 9-208-1 and TM 9-247. For specific cleaning procedures refer to paragraph 8-lOa. On those component parts which contain a hard carbon residue it may be necessary to clean the parts with carbon removing compound, P-C-lll. Observe the following procedures when using P-C-lll.

Warning. *Avoid skin contact with P-C-lll. The compound should be washed off thoroughly with running water if it comes in contact with the skin. A good lanolin base cream, after exposure to the compound, is helpful. The use of rubber gloves and protective equipment is recommended.*

(1) Using a suitable container, fill with fresh compound.

(2) Before soaking parts in the compound, remove all loose dirt, grease, and oil. Place parts to be cleaned in the container, making certain they are completely immersed.

(3) Depending on the amount of residue to be removed, soak for 2 to 16 hours.

(4) Rinse parts with water and dry cleaning solvent (SD), and brush with a stiff bristle brush.

(5) Wipe parts dry and lubricate (par 8-8 and 8-4).

b. Inspection.

Warning. *Clear the weapon of all ammunition before starting an inspection. Remove the magazine and check the chamber to insure it is empty. Do NOT actuate the trigger until the weapon has been cleared.*

Refer to table 3-5 for inspection and repair procedures.

c. Repair.

(1) Remove burs, rough spots, rust and scored areas with a fine stone or crocus cloth moistened with oil. When stoning, care must be taken not to alter any surfaces from the original dimensions.

(2) Replace only those parts which are authorized to organizational maintenance personnel. (Refer to appendix B.)

(3) For repair or replacement of parts, not authorized for organizational maintenance, return pistol to direct support personnel.

(4) For specific repair functions refer to table 3-5.

Table 3-5. Inspection and Repair Procedures

Component Part or Assembly	Inspection	Repair	Reference
Pistol	Overall Condition		
	Nicks, Scratches & Burs	Stone or use crocus cloth.	Para 3-12c (1)
	Rust or Dirt	Clean and lubricate	Para 3-12a, 3-3, & 3-4
	Check Safety & Disconnector tests		Table 3-2
Magazine Assembly	Rust or Dirt	Clean and lubricate	Para 3-12a, 3-3, & 3-4
	Proper assembly	Assemble properly	Para 3-9 & 3-11
	Dull black finish, damaged parts, and proper functioning	Replace Magazine assembly	1, fig B-1
Slide Group	Damaged Parts	Replace only items 8, 9, 11, 12, fig B-1, if damaged.	Para 3-12c (2)
	Inspect for weak extractor: *Note. A weak extractor can readily be detected without disassembly of the slide group as follows: 1. With the tip of the forefinger check for movement of the extractor within the slide, at the ejection part. 2. If the extractor exhibits a side to side movement, the spring tension of the extractor body is weak and the extractor should be replaced*	Replace weak extractor	
	Care must be exercised to preclude forceful ejection of the recoil spring and/or plug as the barrel bushing is turned during disassembly. Spring will not exhibit weakness, distortion or kinks. There will be no flat surfaces		Para 3-12c (3)

	on the coil contour. Uniform diameter of all coils is permissible. A "flat" appearance on either end of the half-coil is not required.		
	Check for loose sights		Para 3-12c (3)
Receiver Group	Rust, dirt or foreign matter	Clean and lubricate	Para 3-12a, 3-3, & 3-4
	Damaged Parts	Replace only items 18, 22, 26, 27, 28, and 80, fig B-1, if Damaged	Par 3-12c (2) and (3)
Holster	Rust, dirt or foreign matter	Clean and lubricate	Para 3-12a, 3-3, & 3-4
	Leather will be soft and pliable, free from tears, cute and cracks. Stitching will be secure and must have all snaps, hooks and pads in place.	Leather material after being water soaked should be cleaned with saddle soap after drying in the shade. Apply mildew preservative leather dressing for field treatment	3 or 4, fig B-2

Note: Brass portion and surrounding leather will be free of green or bluish deposit. leather will be black.

CHAPTER 4 AMMUNITION

4-1. General

Ammunition for the Caliber .45 Automatic Pistol, M1911A1 is issued in the form of a complete round. A complete round (cartridge) consists of all the components (cartridge case, bullet, propellant powder, and primer) necessary to fire the weapon once.

4-2. Classification and Identification of Ammunition

The contents of original boxes or containers can be identified by markings on the box. These markings indicate the number of cartridges in the container, the caliber, the type, the code symbol, and the lot number. The types, uses, and means of identification of ammunition for use in the pistol are:

a. Cartridge, Caliber .45, Ball, M1911, is for use against personnel and light material targets. The ball bullet consists of a metal jacket surrounding a lead alloy core. The bullet tip is unpainted.

b. Cartridge, caliber .45, Blank, M9 is used to simulate fire and for salutes. Due to the configuration of this cartridge it cannot be fired semi-automatically in the pistol and must be used for single shot only. It can be identified by the tapered mouth and absence of a bullet.

c. Cartridge, Caliber .45, Dummy, M1921, is used for training personnel in the -operation of loading and unloading the pistol, and for testing weapons. This cartridge can be identified by the empty primer pocket and two holes in the cartridge case.

d. Cartridge, Caliber .45, Tracer, M26 is used for observation of fire. Secondary uses are for incendiary effect and for signaling. The bullet consists of three parts: a copper-plated or gilding metal-clad steel jacket, a slug of lead hardened with antimony and a tracer mixture in the rear portion of the jacket The bullet is painted red for a distance of approximately 3/16 inch from the tip.

e. Cartridge, Caliber .45, High Density Shot, XM261 is used against personnel. It employs 16 spheres incased in a sabot similar in shape to the ball bullet

CHAPTER 5 DEMOLITION TO PREVENT ENEMY USE

5-1. General

a. Destruction of the pistol when subject to capture or abandonment in the combat zone, will be undertaken only when in the judgment of the commander concerned such action is necessary. If destruction is resorted to, the equipment must be so badly damaged that it cannot be restored to a usable condition in the combat zone either by repair or cannibalization. The reporting of the destruction of equipment is to be through regular channels.

b. Priorities for destruction of parts are:

(1) Firing pin

(2) Barrel

(3) Slide assembly w/sights

(4) Receiver

c. The same priority for the destruction of component parts of the pistol are to be given to the destruction of similar components in spare parts storage areas.

APPENDIX A: REFERENCES

A-1. Publication Index

The following indexes should be consulted frequently for the latest changes or revision of references given in this appendix and for new publications relating to material covered in this manual.

Military Publications:

Index of Administrative Publications DA Past 810-1
Index of Army Films, Transparencies, GTA Charts, and Recordings DA Past 108-1
Index of Doctrinal, Training and Organizational Publications DA Past 810-8
Index of Technical Manuals, Technical Bulletins, Supply Manuals (types 7, 8 DA Past 810-4 and 9) Supply Bulletins and Lubrication Orders

A-2. Forms

DA Form 2028, Recommended Changes to DA Publications
DA Form 2407, Maintenance Request
DD Form 6, Report of Damage or Improper Shipment

A-3. Other Publications

The following explanatory publications pertain to this material.
a. General.
Pistols and Revolvers
Army Equipment Record Procedures
b. Cleaning.
Cleaning of Ordnance Materiel
c. Safety.
Accident Reporting and Records

APPENDIX B: BASIC ISSUE ITEMS LIST AND ORGANIZATIONAL MAINTENANCE REPAIR PARTS AND SPECIAL TOOLS LIST

SECTION I. INTRODUCTION

B-1. Scope

This appendix lists basic issue items, repair parts and special tools required for the performance of organizational maintenance of the Caliber .45 Automatic Pistol, M1S11A1 with hip holster and Caliber .45 Automatic Pistol, M1911A1 with shoulder holster.

B-2. General

This Basic Issue Items, Repair Parts, and Special Tools List is divided into the following sections:

a. Basic Issue Items — Section II. A list of items which accompany the pistols.

b. Maintenance and Operating Supplies — Section III. A listing of maintenance and operating supplies required for initial operation.

c. Prescribed Load Allowance (PLA) — Section IV. A composite listing of repair parts and special tools having quantitative allowances for initial stockage at the organizational level.

d. Repair Parts — Section V. A list of repair parts authorized for the performance of maintenance at the organizational level in figure and item number sequence.

e. Special Tools and Support Equipment — Section VI. A list of special tools and support equipment authorized for the performance of maintenance at the organizational level.

f. Federal Stock Number and Reference Number Index— Section VII. A list of Federal stock numbers in ascending numerical sequence, followed by a list of reference numbers appealing in all the listings, in ascending alpha-numeric sequence, cross-referenced to the illustration figure number and item number.

B-3. Explanation of Columns

The following provides an explanation of columns in the tabular lists in Sections II through VI.

a. Source, Maintenance, and Recoverability Codes (SMR).

(1) Source Code. Indicates the selection status and source for the listed item. Source code used is:

Code	Explanation
P	Applied to repair parts which are stocked in or supplied from Army supply system.

(2) Maintenance Code. Indicates the lowest category of maintenance authorized to install the listed item. The maintenance level codes are:

Code	Explanation
C	Operator/crew
O	Organizational

(3) Recoverability Code. Indicates whether unserviceable items should be returned for recovery or salvage. Items not coded are expendable. Recoverability code is:

Code	Explanation
R	Applied to repair parts and assemblies which are economically reparable and are furnished by supply on an exchange basis.

b. Federal Stock Number. Indicates the Federal stock number assigned to the item and will be used for requisitioning purposes.

c. Description. Indicates the Federal item name and any additional description of the item required. The abbreviation "w/e" when used as a part of the nomenclature, indicates the Federal stock number includes all armament, equipment, accessories and repair parts issued with the item. A part number or other reference number is followed by the applicable five-digit Federal supply code for manufacturers in parentheses.

d. Unit of Measure (U/M). A 2-character alphabetic abbreviation indicating the amount or quantity of the item upon which the allowances are based, e.g., ft, ea, pr, etc.

e. Quantity Incorporated in Unit. Indicates the quantity of the item used in the functional group.

f. Quantity Furnished with the Equipment. Indicates the quantity of an item furnished with the equipment (BIIL only).

g. Component Application. Identifies the component application of each maintenance or operating supply item (M & 0 supplies only).

h. Quantity Required for Initial Operation. Indicates the quantity of each maintenance or operating supply item required for initial operation of the equipment (M & 0 supplies only).

i. Quantity Required for 8 Hours Operation. Indicates the estimated quantities required for an average 8 hours of operation (M & 0 supplies only).

j. Notes. Indicates informative notes keyed to data appearing in a preceding column (M & O supplies only).

k. 15-Day Organizational Maintenance Allowances.

(1) The allowance columns are divided into four sub columns. Indicated in each sub column opposite the first appearance of each item is the total quantity of items authorized for the number of pieces of equipment supported. Subsequent appearances of the same item will have the letters "REF" in the allowance columns. Items authorized for use as required but not for initial stockage are identified with an asterisk in the allowance column.

(2) The quantitative allowances for organizational level of maintenance represents one initial load for a 15-day period for the number of pieces of equipment supported. Units and organizations authorized additional prescribed loads will multiply the number of prescribed loads authorized by the quantity of repair parts reflected in the appropriate density column to obtain the total quantity of repair parts authorized.

(3) Organizational units providing maintenance for more than 100 of these pieces of equipment shall determine the total quantity of parts required by converting the equipment quantity to a decimal factor by placing a decimal point before the next to last digit of the number to indicate hundredths, and multiplying the decimal factor by the parts quantity authorized in the 51-100 allowance column. Example, authorized allowance for 51-100 pieces of equipment is 12; for 140 pieces of equipment multiply 12 by 1.40 or 16.80 rounded off to 17 parts required.

(4) Subsequent changes to allowances will be limited as follows: No change in the range of items is authorized. If additional items are considered necessary, recommendation should be forwarded to Commanding General, Head- quarters, U.S. Army Weapons Command, ATTN: AMSWE-SMM-SA, Rock Island, Illinois 61201, for exception or revision to the allowance list Revisions to the range of items authorized will be made by the U.S. Army Weapons Command based upon engineering experience, demand data, or TAERS Information.

I. Illustration.

(1) Figure Number. Indicates the figure number of the illustration in which the item is shown.

(2) Item Number. Indicates the call-out number used to reference the item in the illustration.

B-4. Special Information

Identification of the usable on codes of this publication are:

Parts without any code are used on either the Pistol, Caliber .45, Automatic M1911AI with Hip Holster or Pistol, Caliber .45, Automatic M1911A1 with Shoulder Holster.

Code	Used on
A	Pistol, Caliber .45, Automatic, M1911A1 with hip holster

only.

B	Pistol, Caliber .45, Automatic, M1911A1 with shoulder

holster only.

B-5. How to Locate Repair Parts

a. When Federal stock number or reference number is unknown:

(1) First. Find illustration B-l covering the Caliber .45 Automatic Pistol, M19UA1.

(2) Second. Identify the repair part on the illustration and figure and item number of the repair part.

(3) Third. Using the Repair Parts Listing locate the illustration figure and item number noted on the illustration.

b. When Federal stock number or reference number is known:

(1) First. Using the Index of Federal Stock Numbers and Reference Numbers find the pertinent Federal stock number or reference number. This index is in ascending FSN sequence followed by a list of reference numbers in alpha-numeric sequence, cross-referenced to the illustration figure number and item number.

(2) Second. Using the Repair Part Listing, find the illustration figure number and item number referenced in the Index of Federal Stock Numbers and Reference Numbers.

B-6. Abbreviations

Abbreviation	Explanation
fil-hd	American National Special Thread
NS	American National Special Thread
o/a	Over-all
phos-ctd	phosohate-coated
S	Steel

B-7. Federal Supply Codes for Manufacturers

Code	Manufacturer
19204	Rock Island Arsenal Rock Island, 111. 61201
19205	Springfield Armory Springfield, Mass. 01101
78277	E.F. Houghton and Co SOS W. Lehigh Ave Philadelphia, Pa. 19188
81848	Federal Specifications
81849	Military Specification
98808	Bray Oil Co 8844 Medford St Los Angeles, Calif. 90068

SECTION II. BASIC ISSUE ITEMS LIST

Basic Issue Items List									
Source, Maint. & Recov. Code			Federal Stock Number	Description	Unit of Measure	Qty. inc. in Unit	Qty. Furn. with Equip.	Illus-tration	
Source	Maintenance	Recovery						Fig. #	Item #
P	C		1005-550-3694	Magazine, Cartridge	EA	1	2	B-1	1
			1005-550-4036	Brush, Cleaning, Small	EA	*****	1	B-2	1
			1005-556-4102	Rod, Cleaning, Small Arms	EA	*****	1	B-2	2
			1095-592-6491	Holster, Pistol: Hip, M1916 (black)	EA	*****	1	B-2	3
			1095-973-2353	Holster, Pistol: Shoulder, M7 (black)	EA	*****	1	B-2	4

SECTION III. MAINTENANCE AND OPERATING SUPPLIES

General Application – 1005-288-3565 – Swab, Small Arms, Cleaning – (1000 per package)

SECTION IV. PRESCRIBED LOAD ALLOWANCE

Prescribed Load Allowance							
Federal Stock Number	Description	QTY Inc. in Unit Pack	15-Day Organizational Maintenance Allowance			
			1-5	6-20	21-30	51-100
1005-501-3198	Link, Barrel	5	**	**	**	2
1005-550-3694	Magazine, Cartridge	1	**	**	2	2
1005-288-3565	Swab, Small Arms, Cleaning	1	**	**	**	2
1005-550-4036	Brush, Cleaning, Small Arms	10	**	**	2	2
1005-556-4102	Rod, Cleaning, Small Arms	1	**	**	**	2
5305-601-9023	Screw, Machine	20	**	**	**	2
5315-501-3199	Pin, Straight, Headless	10	**	**	**	2

Repair Parts List

Source, Maint. & Recov. Code			Federal Stock Number	Description	Unit of Measure	Qty. inc. in Unit	Qty. Furn. with Equip.	15-Day Organizational Maintenance Allowance				Ilustration	
Src	Mnt	RCV						1-5	6-20	21-30	51-100	Fig. #	Item #
Repair parts for: Pistol, CAL .45, Automatic, M1911A1													
P	C		1005-550-3694	Magazine, Cartridge	EA	1	1	*	*	2	2	B-1	1
P	O		5315-501-3199	Pin, Straight, Headless: S, 0.1595 MAX	EA	*	1	*	*	*	2	B-1	8
P	O		1005-501-3198	Link, Barrel	EA	*	1	*	*	*	2	B-1	9
P	O		1005-600-3599	Pin, Firing	EA	*	1	*	*	*	*	B-1	11
P	O		1005-501-3204	Spring, Helical, Compression: 40 coils, firing pin	EA	*	1	*	*	*	*	B-1	12
P	O		1005-600-8602	Spring, Sear	EA	*	1	*	*	*	*	B-1	18
P	O		1005-600-8600	Strut, Hammer	EA	*	1	*	*	*	*	B-1	22
P	O		5305-601-9023	Screw, Machine: fil-hd, S, phos-ctd	EA	*	1	*	*	*	2	B-1	26
P	O		1005-556-4063	Grip, Pistol, LH	EA	*	1	*	*	*	*	B-1	27

P	O		1005-556-4062	Grip, Pistol, RH	EA	*	1	*	*	*	*	B-1	28
P	O		1005-501-3194	Spring, Helical, Compression: 14 1/2 coils, Plunger	EA	*	1	*	*	*	*	B-1	30

SECTION VI. SPECIAL TOOLS LIST

Special Tools List											
Source, Maint. & Recov. Code			Federal Stock Number	Description	Unit of Measure	Qty. inc. in Unit	15-Day Organizational Maintenance Allowance				Ilustration	
Src	Mnt	RCV					1-5	6-20	21-30	51-100	Fig. #	Item #
Tools and Equipment Authorized for Unit Replacement												
			1005-298-3565	Swab, Small Arms, Cleaning: Cotton	P G	*	*	*	*	2		
			1005-550-4036	Brush, Clening, Small Arms: M5 Bore	E A	*	*	*	2	2	B-2	1
			1005-556-4102	Rod, Cleaning, Small Arms: M4	E A	*	*	*	*	2	B-2	2
			1095-592-6491	Holster, Pisto:, Hip, M1916 (black)	E A	*	*	*	*	*	B-2	3
			1095-973-2353	Holster, Pistol: Shoulder, M7 (black)	E A	*	*	*	*	*	B-2	4

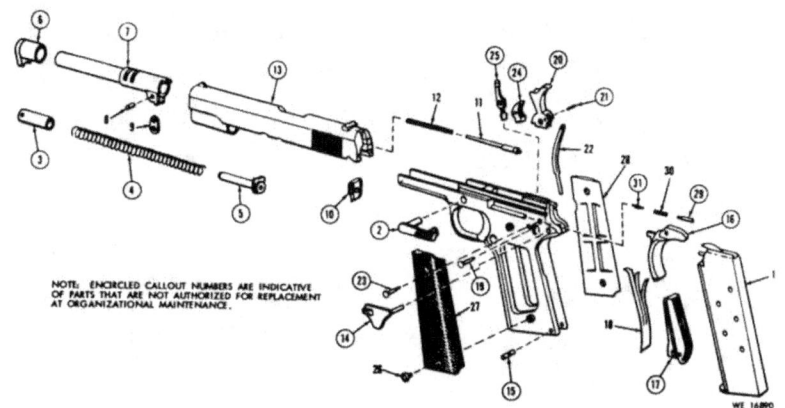

NOTE: ENCIRCLED CALLOUT NUMBERS ARE INDICATIVE OF PARTS THAT ARE NOT AUTHORIZED FOR REPLACEMENT AT ORGANIZATIONAL MAINTENANCE.

Figure B-1 Caliber .45, Automatic, Pistol, M1911A1 - partial exploded view

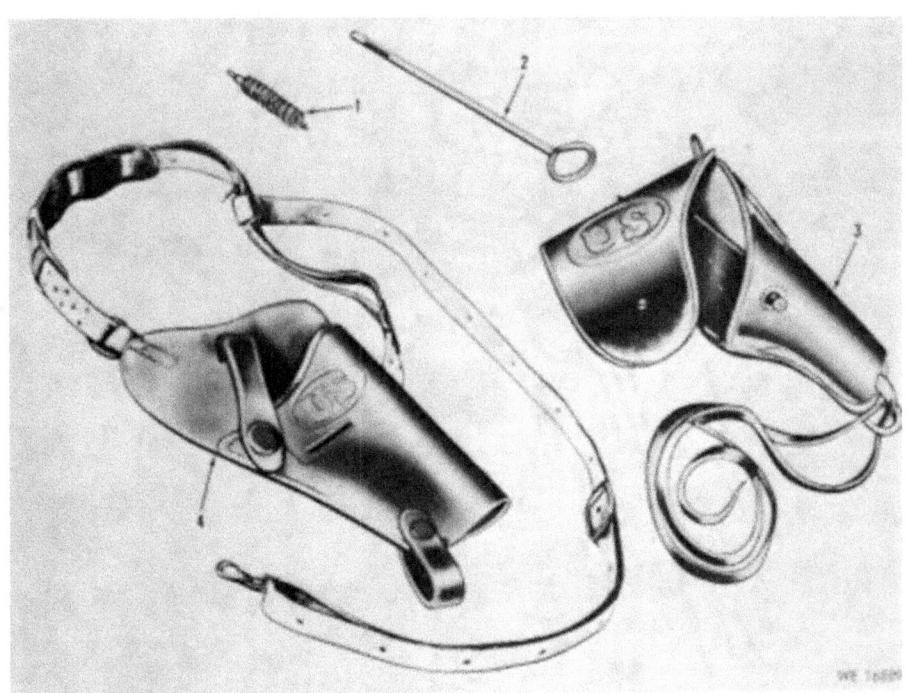

Figure B-2 Special Tools and Equipment

SECTION VIII. FEDERAL STOCK NUMBER AND PARTNUMBER CROSS REFERENCE TO FIGURE AND ITEM NUMBER

Editor's Note: This section has been omitted from this edition because civilians cannot order parts from the military system anyway and the federal supply system has been revamped since the publication of this manual.

APPENDIX C: MAINTENANCE ALLOCATION CHART

SECTION I. INTRODUCTION

C-1. General

The maintenance allocation chart indicates specific maintenance operations performed at proper maintenance levels. Deviation from maintenance operations allocated in the chart is authorized only upon approval of the Commanding Officer.

C-2. Maintenance Functions

The maintenance allocation chart designates overall responsibility for the maintenance function of an end item of assembly. Maintenance functions will be limited to and defined as follows:

INSPECT   To determine serviceability of an item by comparing its physical and mechanical characteristics with established standards.

TEST   To verify serviceability and to detect electrical or mechanical failure by use of test equipment

SERVICE   To dean, preserve and lubricate.

ADJUST   To rectify to the extent necessary to bring into proper operating range.

ALIGN   To adjust specified variable elements of an item to bring to optimum performance.

CALIBRATE   To determine the corrections to be made in the readings of instruments or test equipment used in precise measurement Consists of the comparison of two instruments, one of which is a certified. standard of known accuracy, to detect and adjust any discrepancy in the accuracy of the instrument being compared with the certified standard.

INSTALL   To set up for use in an operational environment

REPLACE   To replace unserviceable items with serviceable assemblies, subassemblies, or parts.

REPAIR   To restore an item to a serviceable condition. This includes, but is not limited to, inspection, cleaning, preserving, adjusting, replacing, welding, riveting, and strengthening.

OVERHAUL   To restore an item to a completely serviceable condition by disassembling the item to determine the condition of each of its component parts and reassembling it using serviceable or new assemblies, subassemblies or parts.

REBUILD   To restore an item to a standard as nearly as possible to original or new condition in appearance, performance, and life expectancy. This is accomplished through complete disassembly of the item, inspection of all parts or components, repair or replacement of worn or unserviceable elements (items) using original manufacturing tolerances and specifications, and subsequent reassembly of the item.

C-3. Explanation of Format

Purpose and use of the format are as follows:

a. *Column a, Group Number.* Lists group numbers, to identify components and assemblies.

b. *Column b, Component Assembly Nomenclature.* Lists the noun names of groups and assemblies on which maintenance is authorized.

e. *Column c, Maintenance Functions.* Lists the various categories of maintenance to be performed on the weapon.

d. *Use of Codes.* Explanation of the use of codes in maintenance function, column c, is as follows:

Code	*Explanation*
C	Operator/Crew
O	Organizational Maintenance
F	Direct Support Maintenance
H	General Support Maintenance
D	Depot Maintenance

e. *Column d, Tools and Equipment.* This column will be used to specify those tools and test equipment required to perform the designated function.

f. *Column e, Remarks.* Self-explanatory.

Note: *Columns not utilized are considered not applicable.*

SECTION II. MAINTENANCE ALLOCATION CHART

Maintenance Allocation Chart													
	Maintenance Function												
Functional Group	Inspect	Test	Service	Adjust	Align	Calibrate	Install	Replace	Repair	Overhaul	Rebuild	Tools & Equipment	Remarks
Pistol, Cal. .45 Automatic, M1911A1	*	F	*	*	*	*	*	*	*	D	*		
Magazine, Cartridge	C	*	C	*	*	*	C	C	*	*	*		
Stop, Slide	*	*	C	*	*	*	C	F	*	*	*		
Slide Group	C	*	C	*	*	*	C	*	O	*	*		
Receiver Group	C	*	C	*	*	*	*	*	O	*	*		

End of TM 9-1005-21--12

OPERATOR AND ORGANIZATIONAL MAINTENANCE
MANUAL
INCLUDING BASIC ISSUE ITEMS LIST
AND REPAIR PARTS AND SPECIAL TOOLS LIST

PISTOL, CALIBER .45, AUTOMATIC, M1911A1 # WITH
HOLSTER, HIP (1005-673-7965) AND PISTOL, CALIBER
.45, AUTOMATIC, M1911 A1, WITH HOLSTER,
SHOULDER (1005-561-2003)

TM 9-1005-211-35

Technical Manual
No. 9-1005-211-35

HEADQUARTERS,
DEPARTMENT OF THE ARMY
Washington, D.C., 18 September 1988

DIRECT SUPPORT, GENERAL SUPPORT, AND DEPOT MAINTENANCE MANUAL INCLUDING REPAIR PARTS AND SPECIAL TOOL LISTS

PISTOL, CALIBER .45, AUTOMATIC: M1911A1, WITH HOLSTER, HIP, W/ E (1005-673-7961) AND PISTOL, CALIBER .45, AUTOMATIC: M1911A1, WITH HOLSTER, SHOULDER, W /E (1005-561-2003)

INCORPORATING CHANGES 1-4
This manual is current as of 28 November 1975

SAFETY PRECAUTIONS	
WARNING	REFERENCE
Before starting an inspection, be sure to clear the weapon. DO NOT actuate the trigger until the weapon has been cleared. Inspect the chamber, to ensure that it is empty, and check to see that no ammunition is in position to be introduced (magazine). Avoid having live ammunition in the vicinity of work area.	Para. 2-6

CHAPTER 1 – INTRODUCTION

SECTION I. GENERAL

1-1. Scope

These instructions are in accordance with the MAC and are published for the use of direct support, general support, and depot maintenance personnel maintaining the Caliber .45, Automatic, Pistol M1911A1. They provide information on the maintenance of the equipment which is beyond the scope of the tools, equipment, personnel or supplies normally available to operator's and organizational maintenance.

Note. All maintenance data, repair parts and special tools and equipment in this manual are used to maintain Caliber .45 Pistol M1911; as applicable.

1-2. Forms and Records

a. General. DA Forms and procedures used for equipment maintenance will be only those prescribed in TM 38-750, Army Equipment Record Procedures.

b. Recommendations for Equipment Publication Improvements. Report of errors, omissions, and recommendations for improving this publication by the individual user is encouraged. Reports should be submitted on DA Form 2028 (Recommended Changes to DA Publications) and forwarded direct to the Commanding General, Headquarters, U.S. Army Weapons Command, ATTN: AMSWESMM-P, Rock Island Arsenal, Rock Island, Illinois 61201.

SECTION II. DESCRIPTION AND DATA

1-3. Description and Tabulated Data

Refer to TM 9-1005-211-12.

CHAPTER 2 – DIRECT SUPPORT, GENERAL SUPPORT, AND DEPOT MAINTENANCE INSTRUCTIONS

SECTION I. REPAIR PARTS, SPECIAL TOOLS AND EQUIPMENT

2-1. Repair Parts Special Tools and Equipment

Refer to appendix B.

2-2. Improvised Tools

Refer to table 2-1.

Table 2-1 Improvised Tools			
Item	**References**		**Required for:**
	Figure	**Use**	
Fixture, Riveting, Front Sight	Fig. 2-1, 2-2	Fig. 3-1	To rivet front sight in place on slide assembly
Tool, Staking plunger tube	Fig. 2-3	Fig. 3-2	To stake bushing in receiver
Tool, Staking, Bushing	Fig 2-4	Fig. 3-3	To stake plunger tube in receiver

Table 2-1. Improvised Tools

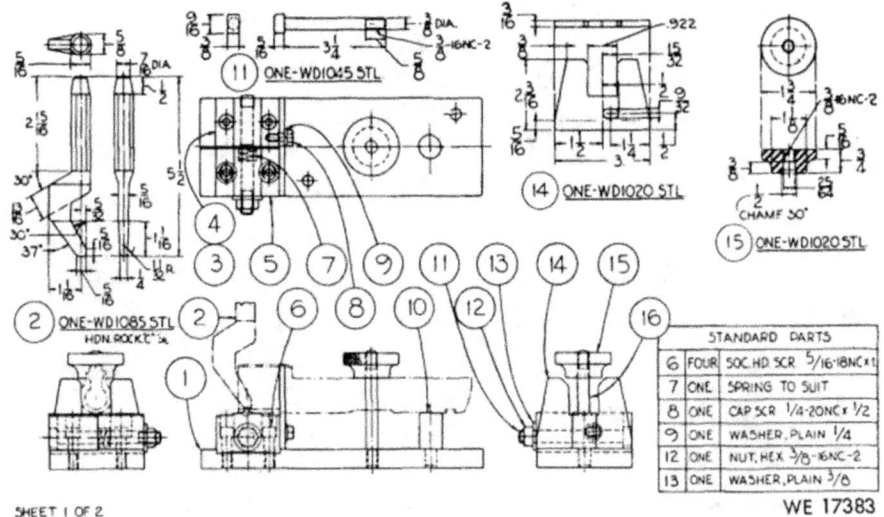

WE 17383

Figure 2-1. Improvised fixture for riveting front sight. (1 of 2)

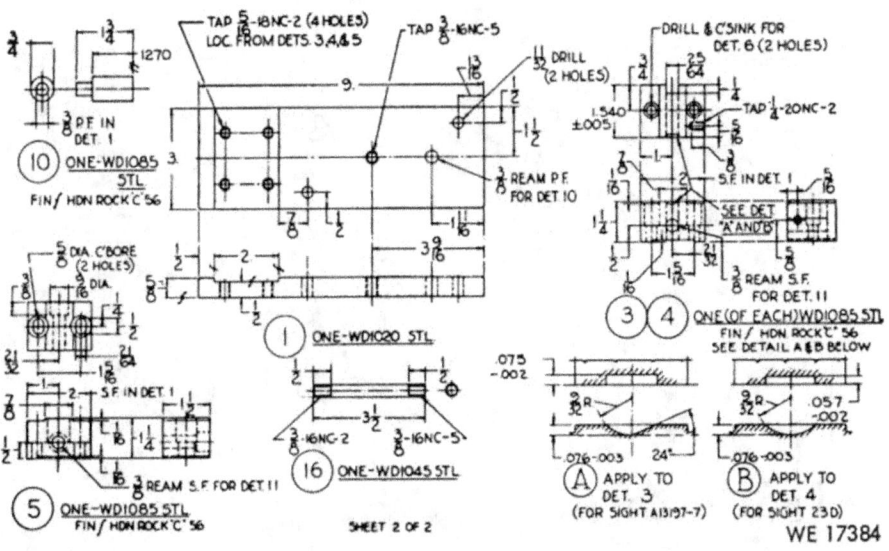

WE 17384

Figure 2-2. Improvised fixture for riveting front sight. (2 of 2)

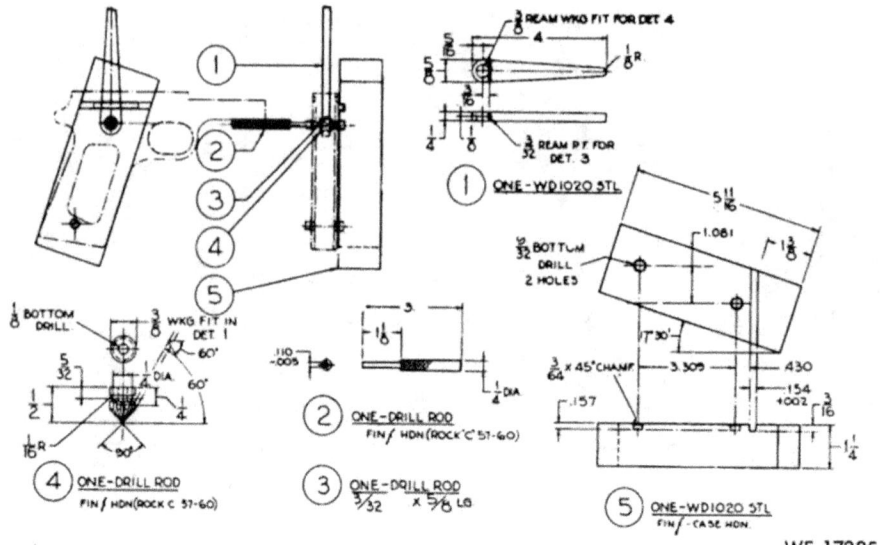

Figure 2-3 Improvised tool for staking bushing.

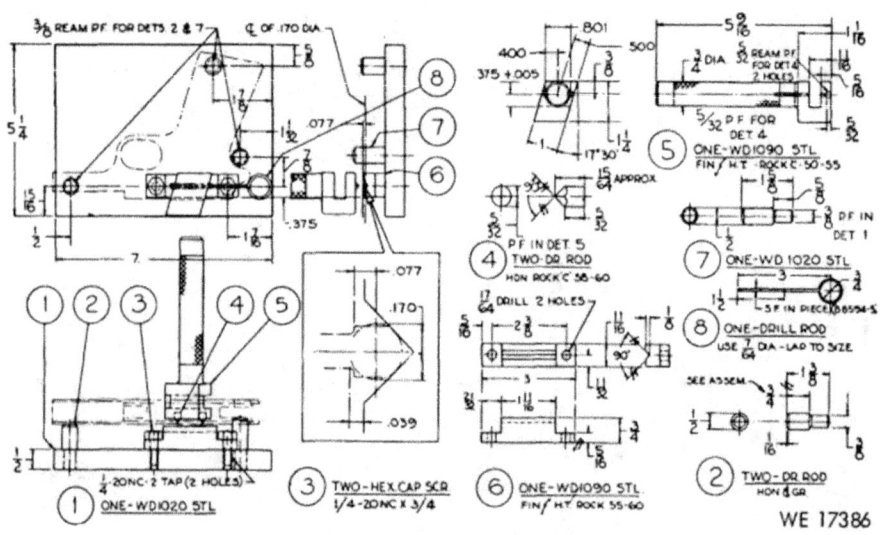

Figure 2-4. Improvised tool for staking plunger tube.

SECTION II. TROUBLESHOOTING

2-3. General

a. Refer to table 2-2.

b. Refer to TM 9-1005-211-12 for operator and organizational troubleshooting procedures.

Table 2-2 Troubleshooting

Malfunction	Probable Cause	Corrective Action
Failure to Feed	Worn or Broken magazine catch	Replace, 20, fig. B-3
Failure to Chamber	Weak Recoil Spring	Replace, 2, fig. B-2
Failure to Lock	Weak Recoil Spring	Replace, 2, fig. B-2
Failure to Fire	Weak Mainspring	Replace, 10, fig. B-3
Failure to Unlock	Broken barrel link lugs	Replace, 10, fig. B-3
Failure to Extract	Broken or worn extractor	Replace extractor, 11, fig. B-2
	Dirty or pitted chamber	Clean chamber, if pitting is excessive, replace barrell, 5 fig. B-3
Failure to Eject	Faulty extractor	Replace extractor, 11, fig. B-2
	Broken ejector	Replace ejector, 25, fig B-3
Failure to Cock	Worn cock notch	Replace hammer, 14, fig B-3
	Worn sear	Replace sear, 18, fig B-3
	Worn or broken disconnector	Replace disconnector, 19, fig B-3
Two shots, or more fired in succession by one trigger squeeze	Worn cock notch	Replace hammer, 14, fig B-3

Table 2-2. Troubleshooting

SECTION III. INSPECTION

2-6. Inspection Procedures

Warning. *Before starting an inspection, be sure to clear the weapon.* DO NOT *actuate the trigger until the weapon has been cleared. Inspect the chamber, to ensure that it is empty, and check to see that no ammunition is in position to be introduced (magazine). Avoid having live ammunition in the vicinity of work area.*

a. Refer to table 2-3 and TM 9-1005-211- 12.

b. Complete inspection of all parts is not always necessary, good judgment should be exercised pertaining to the degree of inspection of integral parts within assemblies.

Table 2-3 Inspection Procedures

Spot Check	Command	Initial	In-process	Pre-embarkation Inspection	Action	Reference
Inspection of materiel in hands of troops		Direct and general support inspections				
X	X	-	-	X	Safety tests and disconnector test.	
X	X			X	Trigger Pull:	**TM 9-1005-211-12, Para 3-5**
X	X	X	X	X	maximum — 6.5 pounds	
X	X	X	X	X	minimum- — 5.0 pounds	
X	X	X	-	X	Magazine assembly	**TM 9-1005-211-12**
					Slide Group	

X	X	X	X	X	Inspect the barrel (5, fig B-2) for burs on exterior and interior rim of the muzzle. Inspect for pitting, bulges, and sharpness of lands. Barrel must be straight, as determined visually, clean and free of corrosion. Pits in the chamber are allowable if they are not large enough to cause extraction difficulties. Pits as wide as a land or groove and less than three-eighths are allowable. Barrels containing pits, as indicated in figure 2-5, will be rejected. Scattered or uniformly fine pits or fine pits in a densely pitted area are allowable. Tool marks or scratches are accepted regardless of length. Tool marks will appear on lines running laterally in the grooves or may run spirally across the top of lands. Definitely ringed bores or bores ringed sufficiently	**fig. 2-5**

					to bulge the outside surface of the barrel are cause for rejection. However, faint rings or shadowy depressions do not indicate an unserviceable barrel and should not be cause for rejection. Barrels will be rejected if worn sufficiently to affect sharpness of the lands. However, pits cutting into lands are acceptable if within the limitations described above. Lands that appear dark due to coating or gilding metal from projectiles should not be cause for rejection.	
X	X	X	X	X	Inspect the barrel bearing for burs and elongation.	**4, fig B-2**
X	X	X	X	X	Inspect slide for breaks or cracks, especially around the ejector port. Inspect the interior grooves and ejector port of slide for excessive wear or burs. Check for loose front or rear sights.	**12, fig B-2**

X	X	X	X	X	Inspect the firing pin for wear or shortness. The pin, as manufactured, has an overall length of 2.290 to 2.296 inches.	**9, fig B-2**
X	X	X	X	X	Inspect the recoil and firing pin springs for damage or deformity. The recoil spring must exhibit a free length of not more than 6⅝ inches or less than 6Vi inches.	**3 & 10, fig B-2**
X	X	X	X	X	Inspect the extractor for wear, weakness, broken lip or deformation.	**11, fig B-2**
X	X	X	X	X	Inspect the recoil spring plug, recoil spring guide, firing pin stop, barrel link and pin for burs or distortions.	**fig B-2**
					Receiver Group	
X	X	X	X	X	Inspect the trigger for burs and wear. Check the half-cock position notch and full-cock notch of hammer for cracks, wear or chips. Make certain the hammer strut is not bent or cracked.	**13, 14, & 16 fig B-3**
X	X	X	X	X	Inspect the sear for worn or	**18, fig B-3**

					chipped tips or worn lugs.	
X	X	X	X	X	Inspect the sear spring for broken leaves, cracks and tension.	**12, fig B-3**
X	X	X	X	X	Inspect disconnector for burs and wear.	**19, fig B-3**
X	X	X	X	X	Inspect the grip safety for burs, wear and cracks on the tip which engages the trigger.	**3, fig B-3**
X	X	X	X	X	Inspect the pin portion and lug of safety for wear or damage.	**3, fig B-3**
X	X	X	X	X	Inspect the mainspring for damage.	**4, fig B-3**
X	X	X	X	X	Inspect the mainspring cap pin, detent plunger and straight-headed pin for burs, wear or damage.	**8, 11, & 9 fig B-3**
X	X	X	X	X	Inspect for bent or worn mainspring housing pin and spring pin.	**2 & 5 fig B-3**
X	X	X	X	X	Inspect slide stop, slide stop plunger and safety plunger for burs, wear or damage.	**2, fig B-1; 32, 30, fig B-3**
X	X	X	X	X	Inspect magazine catch and magazine catch lock for burs and wear. Check magazine spring for damage.	**20 & 21, fig B-3**

X	X	X	X	X	Inspect spring (housing) for burs on mating surfaces, and lanyard loop for being bent, worn or damaged.	**10 & 6, fig B-3**
X	X	X	X	X	Inspect grips for cracks or worn checkering.	**27 & 28, fig B-3**
X	X	X	X	X	Inspect the receiver housing for wear or burs in the slide mating grooves. Inspect the receiver for deformation. Check to see that the plunger tube, ejector, ejector pin, and grip screw bushings are not burred or worn. Check the main spring housing mating grooves in the receiver for burs. Check slide stop notch for oversize or wear.	**34, fig B-3**

Table 2-3. Inspection Procedures

Note. *Recoil spring plugs will not be declared unserviceable when the retaining' tab is damaged or broken. There is no change in weapon functioning or impairment of personnel safety when plugs without tabs are utilized.*

EXAMPLE 1. INTERIOR OF BARREL SHOWING SLIGHT
PITTING AND SHARP LANDS - CUTAWAY VIEW.

EXAMPLE 2. INTERIOR OF BARREL SHOWING
PITTING AND DULL LANDS - CUTAWAY VIEW.

EXAMPLE 3. INTERIOR OF BARREL SHOWING
PITTING, WORN LANDS AND BURS -
CUTAWAY VIEW.

WE 17388

Figure 2-5. Barrel assembly inspection criteria.

SECTION IV. DEPOT MAINTENANCE INSTRUCTIONS

2-7. General

a. For depot maintenance instructions contact the Commanding General, Headquarters, U.S. Army Weapons Command, ATTN: AMSWE-SMM-SA, Rock Island Arsenal, Rock Island, Illinois 61201.

b. Repair parts, special tools and equipment are listed in appendix B of this manual.

CHAPTER 3 – REPAIR INSTRUCTIONS

SECTION I. GENERAL MAINTENANCE

3-1. General

This section provides instructions on general maintenance procedures.

3-2. General Repair Methods

a. Disassembly and Assembly Procedures.

(1) In disassembling the pistol, remove the major groups and assemblies (fig B-l) whenever possible. Groups and assemblies may be disassembled, as necessary, into individual parts.

(2) Complete disassembly of a unit is not always necessary in order to make a required replacement or repair. Good judgment should be exercised to keep disassembly and assembly operations to a minimum.

(3) During assembly, assemblies and groups should be assembled first, then installed to form a complete unit. Lubricate parts before assembly as indicated in TM 9-1005-211-12.

b. Replacement of Parts.

(1) Parts will be replaced when unserviceable.

(2) (Superseded) When assembling a, unit, replace unserviceable pins and screws.

(3) All springs should be replaced if they are broken, deformed, fail to function properly, or fail to meet specific requirements.

(4) If a new part is not available, a reconditioned part may be substituted. Such reconditioned parts should be examined carefully to determine their serviceability.

3-3. Cleaning

Refer to TM 9-1005-211-12 for detailed cleaning procedures.

SECTION II. MAINTENANCE OF CALIBER .45, AUTOMATIC, PISTOL, M1911A1

3-4. General

a. For removal of major groups and assemblies refer to TM 9-1005-211-12 and figure B-l.

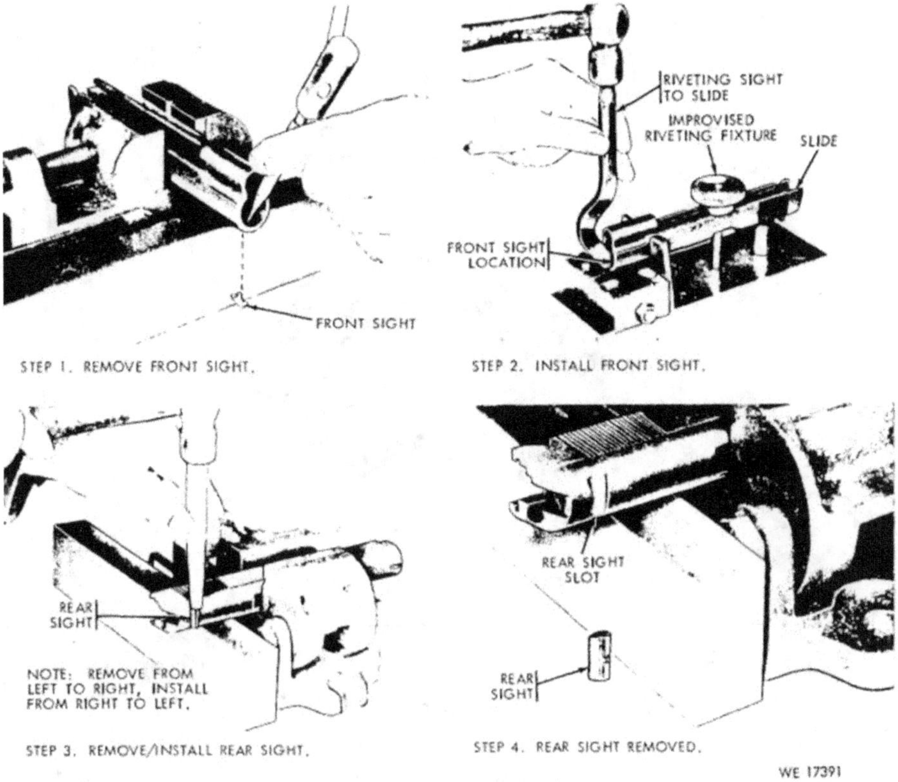

RIVETING SIGHT
TO SLIDE

IMPROVISED
RIVETING FIXTURE   SLIDE

FRONT SIGHT
LOCATION

FRONT SIGHT

STEP 1. REMOVE FRONT SIGHT.   STEP 2. INSTALL FRONT SIGHT.

REAR SIGHT
SLOT

REAR
SIGHT

NOTE: REMOVE FROM
LEFT TO RIGHT, INSTALL
FROM RIGHT TO LEFT.

REAR
SIGHT

STEP 3. REMOVE/INSTALL REAR SIGHT.   STEP 4. REAR SIGHT REMOVED.

WE 17391

Figure 3-1. Removal/installation of front and rear sights and utilizing improvised riveting fixture.

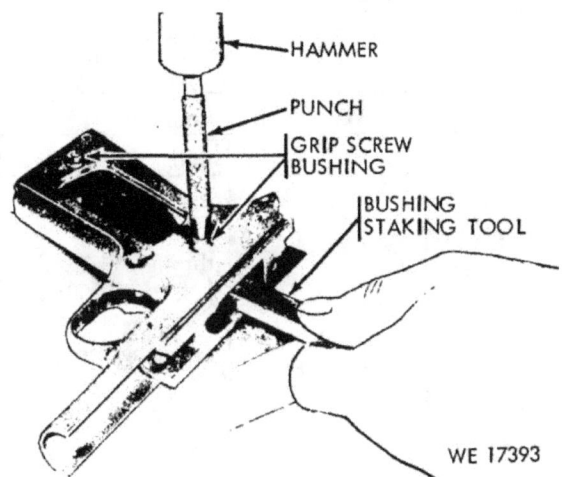

HAMMER

PUNCH

GRIP SCREW
BUSHING

BUSHING
STAKING TOOL

WE 17393

*Figure 3-2. Installing and staking grip screw bushings on receiver, utilizing improvised tool for staking grip
screw bushings.*

63

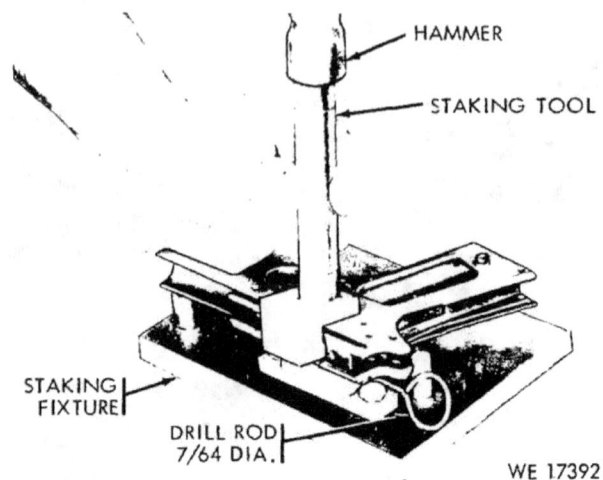

HAMMER

STAKING TOOL

STAKING FIXTURE

DRILL ROD 7/64 DIA.

WE 17392

Figure 3-3. Installing and staking of plunger tube on receiver, utilizing improvised tool for staking plunger tube.

b. Refer to table 3-1 for specific maintenance instructions.

Table 3-1. Guide to Maintenance of Caliber .45 Automatic, Pistol, M1911A1

Groups and assemblies	Disassembly and assembly*	Repair	Tests and adjustments
Caliber .45, Automatic Pistol, M1911A1	TM 9-1005-211-12 and appendix B	Para 3-2	Trigger pull - para 3-5
Magazine Assembly	TM 9-1005-211-12	Replace	
Slide Stop	2, fig B-1	Replace	
Slide Group	Fig B-2	Para 3-2	
		Replace items 1 through 14, fig B-2, if needed. Refer to figure 3-1 for replacing item 14.	
Receiver Group	Fig B-3	Para 3-2	

			Replace items 1 through 33 except 7, figure B-3, if needed. Refer to figure 3-2 for staking item 29 in receiver. Refer to figure 3-3 for staking item 33 on receiver.	

Table 3-1. Guide to Maintenance of Caliber 45 Automatic, Pistol, M1911A1

SECTION III. REPAIR STANDARDS

3-5. Trigger Pull Test

After final assembly of the pistol, check the trigger pull using trigger pull measuring fixture 7274758 (fig 3-4) in accordance with instructions indicated below.

Step 1. With the safety unlocked, rest the weight on the floor and hook the notched portion of the rod over the center portion of the trigger.

Note. Make certain the rod does not contact or rub any portion of the pistol and that rod and barrel are parallel. Empty magazine must be installed when checking the trigger pull.

Step 2. Depress grip safety and carefully raise the weight from the floor. When using the 5-pound weight (minimum), the trigger should not release the hammer. When using the 6.5-pound weight (maximum), the trigger should release the hammer.

Caution: A slow and steady lift must be utilized to assure a true and accurate check.

3-6. Correcting Trigger Pull

Caution. While stoning, critical dimensions should not be altered.

a. Trigger Pull Too Light. This is evidence of a worn cocking notch on the hammer, worn or damaged sear, or a weak helical compression housing spring. Examine the components for wear or damage. If trigger pull cannot be corrected by stoning, replace with new components, as required.

b. Trigger Pull Exercise. This is evidence of burs or surface irregularities on the hammer full-cock notch or sear. A helical compression housing spring that is damaged or too strong and/or interferences or binding between the mating surfaces of the pertinent parts within the receiver group are other probable causes. If the trigger pull cannot be corrected by stoning or changing magazine assemblies, replace with new components, as required.

c. Creep in Trigger. Creep is defined as a perceptible movement of the trigger after the slack has been taken up and before the hammer is released. It is caused by rough or uneven mating surfaces of the sear, hammer, and disconnector and also by unserviceable sear and hammer pins. If the creep cannot be corrected by stoning, replace components, as required.

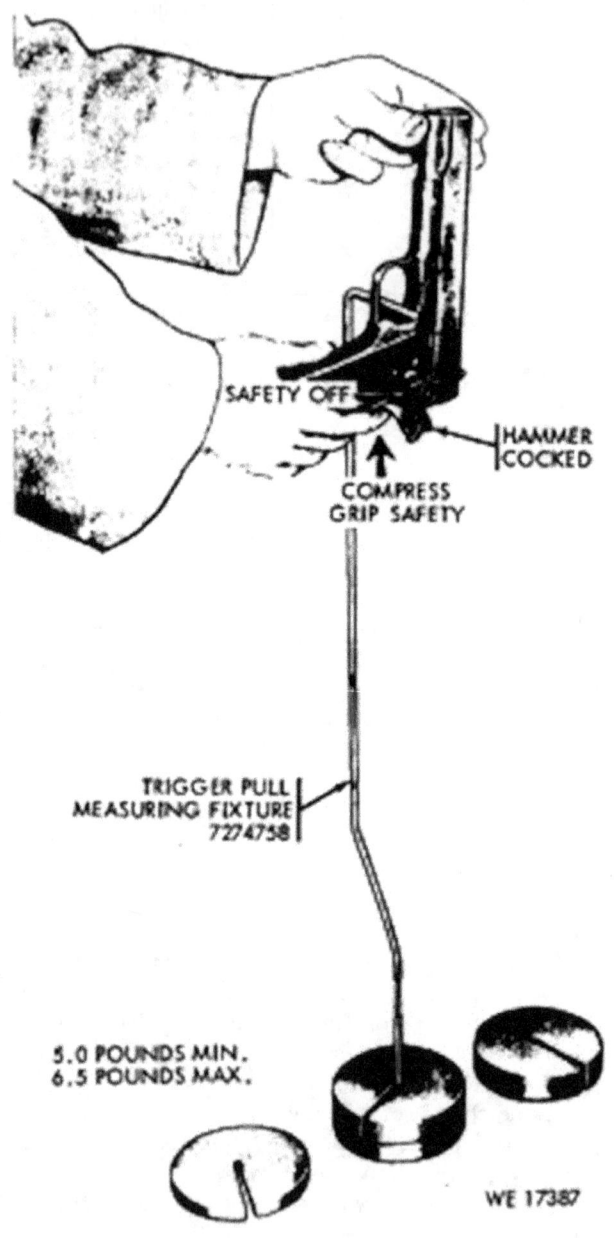

Figure 3-4 Checking trigger pull

CHAPTER 4 – FINAL INSPECTION

4-1. Visual Inspection

For specific visual inspection procedures refer to table 2-8.

4-2. General Functional Inspection

Refer to TM 9-1005-211-12 for procedures in conducting the following: inspections.
a. Check functioning: of safety.
b. Check functioning of grip safety.
c. Check functioning of hammer and sear.
d. Check functioning of disconnector.

4-3. Hand Function Test.

The following hand function test is performed by following the four steps listed below:
Step 1. Place three dummy cartridges in magazine (fig. 4-1, step 1). Insert magazine in receiver group. Release slide stop. This action would cause barrel and slide group to move forward. At the same time, a dummy cartridge will be stripped from magazine into chamber of the weapon.
Step 2. Release safety (Fig 4-1, step 2).
Step 3. Squeeze trigger, allowing hammer to fall (fig. 4-1, step 3). Continue test until third cartridge has been ejected from the pistol, simulating dry firing.
Step 4, When last cartridge is ejected, slide group should remain locked in open position by slide stop (fig 4-4, step 4).

4-4. Function and Firing Tests

Pistols that have been repaired should be function fired, whenever possible, to assure proper operation.

4-5. Corrective Action

Pistols that fail to meet any of the above functional or firing tests are to be corrected by replacement of defective components.

4-6. Completion of Inspection

Upon completion of the final inspection, pistols will be cleaned and lubricated.

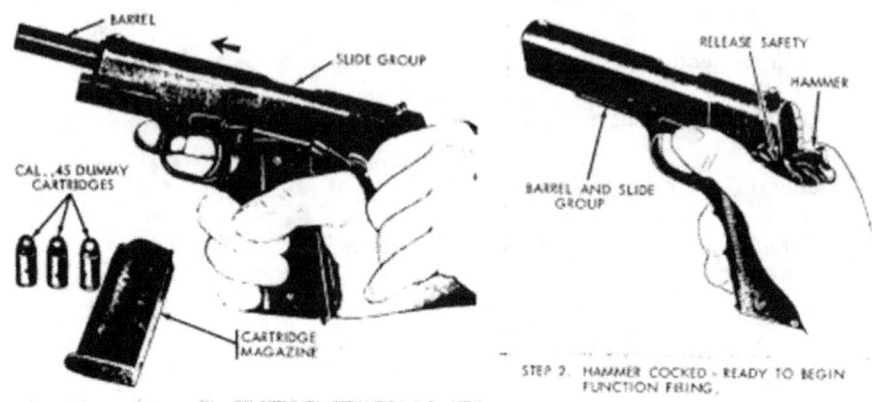

STEP 1. POSITION OF HANDS WHEN LOADING WEAPON - LEFT FRONT VIEW.

STEP 2. HAMMER COCKED - READY TO BEGIN FUNCTION FIRING.

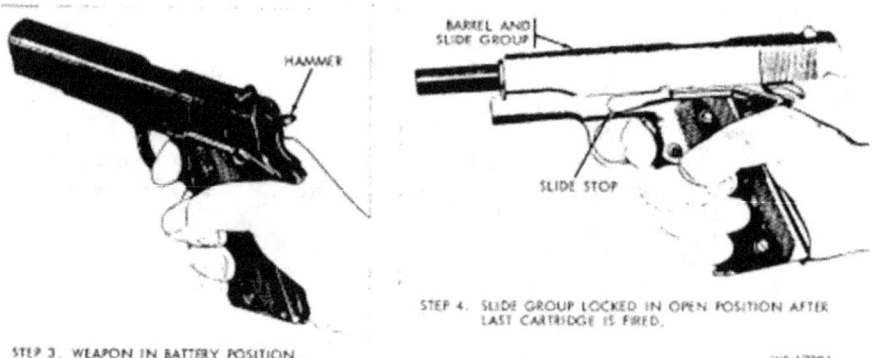

STEP 3. WEAPON IN BATTERY POSITION.

STEP 4. SLIDE GROUP LOCKED IN OPEN POSITION AFTER LAST CARTRIDGE IS FIRED.

WE 17394

Figure 3-5 Hand function test for Caliber 45, Automatic Pistol, M1911A1.

APPENDIX A – REFERENCES

A-1. PUBLICATION INDEXES

The following indexes should be consulted frequently for the latest changes or revisions of references given in this appendix and for new publications relating to material covered in this manual.

Military Publications:

Index of Administrative Publications DA Pam 310-1
Index of Army Films, Transparencies,
GTA Charts and Recording DA Pam 108-1
Index of Blank Forms DA Pam 310-2
Index of Doctrinal Training, and
Organizational Publications DA Pam 310-3
Index of Modification Work Orders DA Pam 310-7
Index of Supply Catalogs and Supply
Manuals (excluding types 7, 8 and 9) DA Pam 310-6
Index of Technical Manuals, Technical
Bulletins, Supply Manuals (types 7, 8 and 9)
Supply Bulletins, and Lubrication Orders DA Pam 310-4

A-2. SUPPLY CATALOGS

Sets, Kits, and Outfits Components List, Tool Set, Direct and General Support Maintenance, Basic Small Arms SC 4933-95-CL-E04

A-3. FORMS

The following form pertains to this materiel.
DA Form 2028, Recommended Changes to DA Publications.

A-4. OTHER PUBLICATIONS

The following explanatory publications pertain to this material,

a. General.

Operator and Organizational Maintenance Manual including Repair Parts and Special Tool Lists for Caliber .45 Automatic Pistol M1911A1 with Hip Holster and Caliber .45 Automatic Pistol M1911A1 with Shoulder Holster TM 9-1005-211-12
Pistols and Revolvers FM 23-35
Army Equipment Record Procedures TM 38-750

b. Cleaning.

Cleaning of Ordnance Materiel TM 9-208-1

c. Inspections.

Command Maintenance Management Inspection AR 750-8
Small Arms Weapons: Standards for Visual
Inspections of Barrels TB ORD 437

d. Issue of Supplies and Equipment.

Requisitioning, Receipt, and Issue System AR 725-50

e. Logistics.

Malfunctions Involving Ammunition and Explosives AR 700-1300-8

f. Maintenance of Supplies and Equipment.

Organization, Policies, and Responsibilities for Maintenance Operations AR
750-5

g. Safety.

Accident Reporting and Records AR 385-40

APPENDIX B – DIRECT SUPPORT, GENERAL SUPPORT, AND DEPOT MAINTENANCE REPAIR PARTS AND SPECIAL TOOLS LIST

SECTION I. INTRODUCTION

B-1. Scope

This appendix is a list of repair parts and special tools required for the performance of direct support, general support, and depot maintenance of the M1911A1, Caliber .45, Automatic, Pistol.

B-2. General

This repair parts and special tools list is divided into the following sections:

a. Repair Parts — Section II. A list of repair parts authorized for the performance of maintenance at the direct support, general support, and depot level in figure and item number sequence.

b. Special Tools, Test and Support Equipment — Section III. A list of special tools, test and support equipment authorized for the performance of maintenance at the direct support, general support, and depot level.

c. Federal Stock Number and Reference Number Index — Section IV. A list of Federal stock numbers in ascending numerical sequence followed by a list of referenced numbers in ascending alpha-numeric sequence, cross-referenced to the illustration figure number and item number.

B-3. Explanation of Columns

The following provides an explanation of columns in the tabular lists in sections II and III:

a. Source, Maintenance, and Recoverability Codes (SMR), Column 1.

(1) Source code, indicates the selection status and source for the listed item. Source codes used are:

Code	Explanation
P	Repair parts which are stocked in or supplied from the GSA, DSA, or Army supply system, and authorized for use at indicated maintenance categories.
M	Repair parts which are not procured or stocked but are manufactured at indicated maintenance categories.
A	Assemblies which are not procured or stocked as such but are made up of two or more units, each of which carry individual FSNs and

descriptions and are procured and stocked and can be assembled by units at indicated maintenance categories.

X   Parts and assemblies which are not procured or stocked; the mortality of which is normally below that of the applicable end item; and the failure of which should result in retirement of the end item from the supply system.

X1   Repair parts which are not procured or stocked, the requirements for which will be supplied by use of next higher assembly or component.

X2   Repair parts which are not stocked. The indicated maintenance category requiring such repair parts will attempt to obtain through cannibalization; if not obtainable through cannibalization, such repair parts will be requisitioned with supporting justification through normal channels.

C   Repair parts authorized for local procurement. When not obtainable from local procurement, such repair parts will be requisitioned through normal supply channels with a supporting statement of non-availability from local procurement.

G   Major assemblies that are procured with PEMA funds for initial issue only to be used as exchange assemblies at DSU and GSU level. These assemblies will not be stocked above DSU and GSU level or returned to Depot supply level.

(2) Maintenance code, indicates the lowest category of maintenance authorized to install the listed item. The maintenance level codes are:

Code	Explanation
C	Operator/crew
O	Organizational Maintenance
F	Direct Support Maintenance
H	General Support Maintenance
D	Depot Maintenance

(3) Recover ability code, indicates whether unserviceable items should be returned for recovery or salvage. Items not coded are expendable. Recoverability codes are:

Code	*Explanation*

R   Repair parts and assemblies which are economically repairable at DSU and GSU activities and are normally furnished by supply on an exchange basis.

T   High dollar value recoverable repair parts which are subject to special handling and are issued on an exchange basis. Such repair parts are normally repaired or overhauled at depot maintenance activities.

U   Repair parts specifically selected for salvage by reclamation units because of precious metal content, critical materials, high dollar value, reusable casings, etc.

S   Repair parts and assemblies which are economically repairable at DSU and GSU activities and normally are furnished by supply on an exchange basis. However, when these items are determined to be uneconomically repairable by a GSU, they will be evacuated to a depot for evaluation and analysis before final disposition.

No Code   Indicated Parts will be considered expendable.

  b. Federal Stock Number, Column 2. This column indicates the Federal stock number assigned to the item and will be used for requisitioning purposes.

  c. Description, Column 3. This column indicates the Federal item name and any additional description of the item required. The abbreviation "w/e" when used as a part of the nomenclature, indicates the Federal stock number includes all armament equipment, accessories, and repair parts issued with the item. A part number or other reference number is followed by the applicable five-digit Federal supply code for manufacturers in parentheses. Repair parts quantities included in the kits, sets, and assemblies are shown in front of the repair part name.

  d. Unit of Measure (U/M), Column U. A 2-character alphabetic abbreviation indicating the amount or quantity of the item upon which the allowances are based, e.g., ft, ea, pr, etc.

  e. Quantity Incorporated in Unit, Column 5. This column indicates the quantity of the item used in a functional group or assembly. A "V" appearing in this column in lieu of a quantity indicates that a definite quantity cannot be indicated (e.g., shims, spacers, etc.).

  f. 30-Day DS/GS Maintenance Allowances, Columns 6, and 7.

  Note. *Allowances in GS column are for GS maintenance only.*

  (1) The allowance columns are divided into three sub columns. Indicated in each sub column, opposite the first appearance of each item, is the total quantity of items authorized for the number of pieces of equipment supported. Subsequent appearances of the same item will have the letters "REF" in the applicable allowance columns. Items authorized for use as required but not for initial stockage are identified with an asterisk in the allowance column.

  (2) The quantitative allowances for DS/ GS levels of maintenance will represent initial stockage for a 30-day period for the number of pieces of equipment supported.

  (3) Determination of the total quantity of parts required for maintenance of more than 100 of these pieces of equipment can be accomplished by converting the

equipment quantity to a decimal factor by placing a decimal point before the next to last digit of the number to indicate hundredths, and multiplying the decimal factor by the parts quantity authorized in the 51-100 allowance column. Example, authorized allowance for 51-100 pieces of equipment is 40; for 150 pieces of equipment multiply 40 by 1.50 or 60 parts required.

g. 1-Year Allowances Per 100 Pieces of Equipment/ Contingency Planning Purposes, Column 8. This column indicates opposite the first appearance of each item the total quantity required for distribution and contingency planning purposes: The range of items indicates total quantities of all authorized items required to provide for adequate support of 100 pieces of equipment for one year.

h. Depot Maintenance Allowance Per 100 Pieces of Equipment, Column 9. This column indicates opposite the first appearance of each item, the total quantity authorized for depot maintenance of 100 pieces of equipment. Subsequent appearances of the same item will have the letters "REF" in the allowance column. Items authorized for use as required but not for initial stockage are identified with an asterisk in the allowance column.

i. Illustration, Column 10. This column is divided as follows:

(1) Figure Number, Column 10a. Indicates the figure number of the illustration in which the item is shown.

(2) Item Number, Column 10b. Indicates the callout number used to reference the item in the illustration.

B-4. Special Information

a. Identification of the usable on codes included in column 3 of this publication are:

Parts without any code are used on either the Pistol, Caliber .45, Automatic, M1911A1 with Hip Holster or Pistol, Caliber .45, Automatic, M1911A1 with Shoulder Holster. A Pistol, Caliber .45, Automatic, M1911A1 with hip holster only.

Code	Used On
	Parts without any code are used on either the Pistol, Caliber .45, Automatic, M1911A1 with Hip Holster or Pistol, Caliber .45, Automatic, M1911A1 with Shoulder Holster.
A	Pistol, Caliber .45, Automatic, M1911A1 with hip holster only.
B	Pistol, Caliber .45, Automatic, M1911A1 with shoulder holster only.

b. The following publications pertain to the Pistol, Caliber .45, Automatic, M1911A1 and its components.

- FM 23-35 Pistols and Revolvers
- TM 9-1005-211-12 Operator's and Organizational Maintenance Manual including Basic Issue Items List, Repair Parts and Special Tools and Equipment Lists.

B-5. How to Locate Repair Parts

a. When Federal stock number or reference number is unknown:

(1) First. Using the table of contents, determine the functional group or assembly within which the repair part belongs. This is necessary since illustrations are prepared for functional groups or assemblies and listings are divided into the same groups.

(2) Second. Find the illustration covering the functional group or assembly to which the repair part belongs.

(3) Third. Identify the repair part on the illustration and note the illustration figure and item number of the repair part.

(4) Fourth. Using the Repair Parts Listing, find the functional group or assembly to which the repair part belongs and locate the illustration figure and item number noted on the illustration.

b. When Federal stock number or reference number is known:

(1) First. Using the Index of Federal Stock Numbers and Reference Numbers find the pertinent Federal stock number or reference number. This index is in ascending FSN sequence followed by a list of reference numbers in ascending alpha-numeric sequence, cross-referenced to the illustration figure number and item number.

(2) Second. Using the Repair Parts Listing, find the functional group or assembly of the repair part and the illustration figure number and item number referenced in the Index of Federal Stock Numbers and Reference numbers.

B-6. Abbreviations

Abbreviations Explanation

cd-pltd - cadmium plated
cham - chamfer
fll-hd - fillister head
fl-ck-hd - flat countersunk head
fl-fil-hd -flat fillister head
o/a -over-all
phos-fin - phosphate finish
S - steel

B-7. Federal Supply Codes for Manufacturers

Code	Manufacturer
19204	Rock Island Arsenal
Rock Island, Illinois	
19205	Springfield Armory
Springfield, Mass.	
96906	Military Standard

SECTION II. REPAIR PARTS LIST

(1) Source, Maint. And Recov. Code			(2) Federal Stock No.	(3) Description	(4) Unit of Issue	(5) Qty. Inc. in Unit	(6) Direct Support 30-Day Maint. Allowance			(7) General Support 30-Day Maint. Allowance			(8) 1 Yr. Alw. Per 100 Equip/Catary Planning	(9) Depot Maint. Alw. Per 100 Equip	(10) Illustration	
(A) Source	(B) Maint.	(C) Recov.					(A) 1-20	(B) 21-50	(C) 51-100	(A) 1-20	(B) 21-50	(C) 51-100			(A) Fig. No.	(B) Item No.
				REPAIR PARTS FOR: PISTOL, CAL. .45, AUTOMATIC, M1911A1 MAJOR GROUPS AND ASSEMBLIES												
P	C		1005-550-8694	MAGAZINE, CARTRIDGE: 5508694 (19205)	EA	1	2	2	2	2	2	2	24	48	B1	1
P	F		1005-600-8595	STOP, SLIDE: 6008595 (19205)	EA	1	•	•	2	•	•	2	24	4	B1	2
A				SLIDE GROUP	---	1	---	---	---	---	---	---	---	---	B1	3
A				RECEIVER GROUP	---	1	---	---	---	---	---	---	---	---	B1	4
				SLIDE GROUP												
P	F		1005-501-3201	PLUG, RECOIL SPRING: 5013201 (19205)	EA	1	•	2	2	•	2	2	24	8	B2	1
P	F		1005-501-3200	SPRING, HELICAL, COMPRESSION: 30 COILS, RECOIL 5013200 (19205)	EA	1	•	2	2	•	2	2	24	8	B2	2
P	F		1005-600-8597	GUIDE, RECOIL SPRING: 6008597 (19205)	EA	1	•	•	2	•	•	2	24	4	B2	3
P	F		1005-600-8596	BEARING, BARREL: 6008596 (19205)	EA	1	•	•	2	•	•	2	24	4	B2	4
P	F		1005-722-3849	BARREL, PISTOL: 7791193 (19205)	EA	1	•	2	2	•	2	2	24	20	B2	5
P	O		5315-501-3199	PIN, STRAIGHT, HEADLESS: S, 0.1555 MAX DIA, 0.358 O/A LG (BARREL LINK) 5013199 (19205)	EA	1	2	2	2	2	2	2	24	15	B2	6
P	O		1005-501-3198	LINK, BARREL: 5013198 (19205)	EA	1	2	2	2	2	2	2	24	5	B2	7
P	F		1005-501-3205	STOP, FIRING PIN: 5013205 (19205)	EA	1	•	•	2	•	•	2	24	10	B2	8
P	O		1005-600-8599	PIN, FIRING: 6008599 (19205)	EA	1	•	•	2	•	•	2	24	5	B2	9
P	O		1005-501-3204	SPRING, HELICAL, COMPRESSION: 40 COILS FIRING PIN 5013204 (19205)	EA	1	•	2	2	•	2	2	24	8	B2	10
P	F		1005-600-8598	EXTRACTOR, SMALL ARMS CARTRIDGE: 6008598 (19205)	EA	1	•	2	2	•	2	2	24	8	B2	10
P	H	R	1005-876-4033	SLIDE, AUTOMATIC PISTOL 7790353 (19205)	EA	1	---	---	---	•	•	2	24	4	B2	12
P	F		1005-501-3196	SIGHT, REAR: S, 0.245 H, 0.626 LG 5013196 (19205)	EA	1	•	•	2	•	•	2	24	4	B2	13
P	F		1005-501-3197	SIGHT, FRONT: 5013197 (19205)	EA	1	•	•	2	•	•	2	24	8	B2	14
X1				SLIDE: 7790314	---	1									B2	15
				RECEIVER GROUP												
P	F		1005-550-3840	SAFETY, SMALL ARMS: 5503840 (19205)	EA	1	•	•	2	•	•	2	24	8	B3	1
P	F		1005-501-3212	PIN, MAINSPRING HOUSING: 5013212 (19205)	EA	1	•	•	2	•	•	2	24	4	B3	2
P	F		1005-650-1828	SAFETY, GUN GRIP: 6501828 (19205)	EA	1	•	•	2	•	•	2	24	4	B3	3
P	D		1005-556-4058	HOUSING, ASSEMBLY, MAINSPRING: 5564058 (19205)	EA	1	---	---	---	---	---	---		5	B3	4
P	F		5315-844-4790	PIN, SPRING: TUBULAR, SLOTTED, BOTH ENDS CHAM, S, CD-PLTD, 0.093 DIA, 0.500 LG, 0.022 STK THK MS 16562-25 (96906)	EA	1	•	•	2	•	•	2	24	2	B3	5
P	F		1005-501-3214	LOOP, LANYARD: U SHAPE, 0.107 STK DIA, 1/2 LG 5013214 (19205)	EA	1	•	•	2	•	•	2	24	2	B3	6
X1				HOUSING, MAINSPRING: 5503841	---	---	---	---	---	---	---	---	---	---	B3	7
P	F		5315-501-3210	PIN, STRAIGHT, HEADED: FL-CK-HD, S, 0.084 SHANK DIA, 9.369 LG (MAIN-SPRING HOUSING) 5013210 (19205)	EA	1	•	•	2	•	•	2	24	4	B3	8
P	F		5315-501-3209	PIN, STRAIGHT, HEADED: FL-FIL-HD, S, 0.174 SHANK DIA, 0.608 LG (MAIN-SPRING CAP) 5013209 (19205)	EA	1	•	•	2	•	•	2	24	4	B3	9
P	F		1005-501-3208	SPRING, HELICAL, COMPRESSION: S, 21.5 COILS, HOUSING ASSY 5013208 (19205)	EA	1	•	2	2	•	2	2	24	5	B3	10
P	F		1005-501-3213	PLUNGER, DETENT: 5013213 (19205)	EA	1	•	•	2	•	•	2	24	4	B3	11
P	O		1005-600-8602	SPRING, SEAR: 6008602 (19205)	EA	1	•	2	2	•	2	2	24	12	B3	12
P	F		5315-501-3206	PIN, STRAIGHT, HEADED: FL-CK-HD, S, 0.157 MAX SHANK DIA, 0.786 LG UNDER HD (HAMMER) 5013206 (19205)	EA	1	•	•	2	•	•	2	24	5	B3	13
P	F		1005-980-1743	HAMMER, FIRING, SMALL ARMS: 7790803 (19205)	EA	1	•	•	2	•	•	2	24	4	B3	14

(1) Source, Maint. And Recov. Code			(2) Federal Stock No.	(3) Description	(4) Unit of Issue	(5) Qty. Inc. In Unit	(6) Direct Support 30-Day Maint. Allowance			(7) General Support 30-Day Maint. Allowance			(8) 1 Yr. Alw. Per 100 Equip/ Category Planning	(9) Depot Maint. Alw. Per 100 Equip	(10) Illustration	
(A) Source	(B) Maint.	(C) Recov.					(A) 1-20	(B) 21-50	(C) 51-100	(A) 1-20	(B) 21-50	(C) 51-100			(A) Fig. No.	(B) Item No.
P	F		5315-501-3207	PIN, STRAIGHT, HEADLESS: S, PHOS-FIN., 0.96 MAX DIA, 0.305 O/A LG (HAMMER STRUT) 5013207 (19205)	EA	1	*	2	2	*	2	2	24	5	B3	15
P	O		1005-600-8600	STRUT, HAMMER: 6008600 (19205)	EA	1	*	*	2	*	2	2	24	4	B3	16
P	F		5315-501-3211	PIN, STRAIGHT, HEADED: FL-CK-HD, S, 0.110 MAX SHAFT DIA, 0.780 MAX LG UNDER HD (SEAR) 5013211 (19205)	EA	1	*	*	2	*	*	2	24	4	B3	17
P	F		1005-592-9974	SEAR: 7268068 (19205)	EA	1	*	2	2	*	2	2	24	16	B3	18
P	F		1005-600-8603	DISCONNECTOR, RECEIVER ASSEMBLY: 6008603 (19205)	EA	1	*	2	2	*	2	2	24	16	B3	19
P	F		1005-600-8609	CATCH, MAGAZINE: 6008609 (19205)	EA	1	*	*	2	*	*	2	24	4	B3	20
P	F		1005-501-3218	LOCK, MAGAZINE CATCH: 5013218 (19205)	EA	1	*	*	2	*	*	2	24	8	B3	21
P	F		1005-501-3217	SPRING, HELICAL, COMPRESSION: 13 COILS MAGAZINE CATCH 5013217 (19205)	EA	1	*	*	2	*	*	2	24	10	B3	22
P	F		1005-614-7780	TRIGGER: 6147780 (19205)	EA	1	*	*	2	*	*	2	24	4	B3	23
P	F		5315-501-3203	PIN, STRAIGHT, HEADLESS: S, 0.063 MAX DIA, 39/64 O/A LG (EJECTOR) 5013203 (19205)	EA	1	*	*	2	*	*	2	24	4	B3	24
P	F		1005-903-8192	EJECTOR, CARTRIDGE: 11010485 (19205)	EA	1	*	*	2	*	*	2	24	4	B3	25
P	O		5305-601-9023	SCREW, MACHINE: FIL-HD, S, PHOS-CTD, 0.150-5 ONS, 6.260 O/A LG (GRIP) 6019023 (19205)	EA	4	2	2	2	2	2	2	24	16	B3	26
P	O		1005-556-4063	GRIP, PISTOL: LH, PLASTIC, CHECKERED 5564063 (19205)	EA	1	*	2	2	*	2	2	24	10	B3	27
P	O		1005-556-4062	GRIP, PISTOL: RH, PLASTIC, CHECKERED 5564062 (19205)	EA	1	*	2	2	*	2	2	24	10	B3	28
P	F		1005-601-9022	BUSHING, STOCK SCREW: RECEIVER ASSY 6019022 (19205)	EA	4	*	*	2	*	*	2	24	8	B3	29
P	F		1005-501-3195	PLUNGER, SAFETY: 5013195 (19205)	EA	1	*	*	2	*	*	2	24	4	B3	30
P	O		1005-501-3194	SPRING, HELICAL, COMPRESSION: 14-1/2 COILS, PLUNGER 5013194 (19205)	EA	1	*	2	2	*	2	2	24	8	B3	31
P	F		1005-501-3193	PLUNGER, SLIDE STOP: 5013193 (19205)	EA	1	*	*	2	*	*	2	24	4	B3	32
P	F		1005-600-8594	TUBE, PLUNGER: 6008594 (19205)	EA	1	*	2	2	*	2	2	24	8	B3	33
X1				RECEIVER: 6535359		1									B3	34

SECTION III. SPECIAL TOOLS, TEST AND SUPPORT EQUIPMENT LIST

(1) Source, Maint. And Recov. Code			(2) Federal Stock No.	(3) Description	(4) Unit of Issue	(5) Qtr. Inc. In Unit	(6) Direct Support 30-Day Maint. Allowance			(7) General Support 30-Day Maint. Allowance			(8) 1 Yr. Alw. Per 100 Equip/ Category Planning	(9) Depot Maint. Alw. Per 100 Equip	(10) Illustration	
(A) Source	(B) Maint.	(C) Recov.					(A) 1-20	(B) 21-50	(C) 51-100	(A) 1-20	(B) 21-50	(C) 51-100			(A) Fig. No.	(B) Item No.
				TOOLS AND EQUIPMENT AUTHORIZED FOR UNIT REPLACEMENT												
			1005-288-3565	SWAB, SMALL ARMS CLEANING: COTTON, 2-1/2 SQ (1000 IN PKG) 5019316 (19204)	PK	....	2	2	2	2	2	2	24			
			1005-556-4036	BRUSH, CLEANING, SMALL ARMS: M5 BORE 5564036 (19205)	EA	...	2	2	2	2	2	2	24			
			1005-556-4102	ROD, CLEANING, SMALL ARMS: M4 5564102 (19205)	EA	...	2	2	2	2	2	2	24			
			1005-592-6491	HOLSTER, PISTOL: HIP, M1916 (BLACK) 7791466 (19205) A OR	EA	...	*	2	2	*	2	2	24			
			1095-973-2353	HOLISTER, PISTOL: SHOULDER, M7, (BLACK) 7791527 (19205) B	EA	...	*	2	2	*	2	2	24			
				TOOLS AND EQUIPMENT THE FOLLOWING ITEMS ARE REQUISITIONED AND ISSUED, IF NOT OTHERWISE AUTHORIZED, TO ORDNANCE MAINTENANCE UNITS PERFORMING MAINTENANCE SUPPORT OF THE MAJOR ITEMS. ITEMS MAY BE REQUISITIONED AS REQUIRED FOR REPLACEMENT UNDER THEIR INDIVIDUAL STOCK NUMBERS. THE 15-DAY LEVEL IS NOT APPLICABLE. THE FOLLOWING BASIC SMALL ARMS DIRECT AND GENERAL SUPPORT MAINTENANCE TOOL SET IS AUTHORIZED, AS REQUIRED, TO ALL MAINTENANCE SUPPORT UNITS WITH A SMALL ARMS REPAIR MISSION.												
	R		4933-775-0366	TOOL SET, DIRECT AND GENERAL SUPPORT MAINTENANCE. BASIC	SE	...	*	*	*	*	*	*				
				SMALL ARMS: 8426358 (19205) NOTE: SEE SC 4933-95-CL-E04 FOR COMPONENTS.												
	R		4933-726-5840	TOOL KIT, PISTOL, AUTOMATIC, CALIBER .45: DEPOT MAINTENANCE 7265840 (19205) COMPOSED OF:	SE									*		
			4933-731-9912	2—GAGE, SNAP, FIXED: NOT GO 0.150, 1-1/4 W, 3/32 THK, 2 LG 7319912 (19205)	EA	..	...	....	....	...	....	...			B4	1
			4933-731-9913	2—GAGE, SNAP, FIXED: NOT GO 0.197, 1-1/4 W, 3/32 THK, 2 LG 7319913 (19205)	EA	..	...	....	....	...	....	...			B4	2
			4933-731-9915	2—GAGE, PLUG, BARREL BUSHING: NOT GO, 0.582 AND 0587 DIA 7319915 (19205)	EA	..	...	....	....	...	....	...			B4	3
			5220-731-9916	2—GAGE, PLUG, PLAIN CYLINDRICAL: SINGLE END NOT GO 0.704 OD 7319916 (19205)	EA	..	...	....	....	...	....	...			B4	4
				SPECIAL PACKAGING MATERIAL THE VOLATILE CORROSION INHIBITOR LISTED BELOW IS REQUIRED WHEN THE MAJOR ITEM IS PACKAGED FOR STORAGE PURPOSES. FIELD REQUIREMENTS FOR PACKAGING THE MAJOR ITEMS ARE REQUISITIONED AS REQUIRED.												
			1005-336-0228	BAG, BARRIER, VCI TREATED LINER: 7265932 (19205)	EA	..	...	....	....	...	....	...		100		

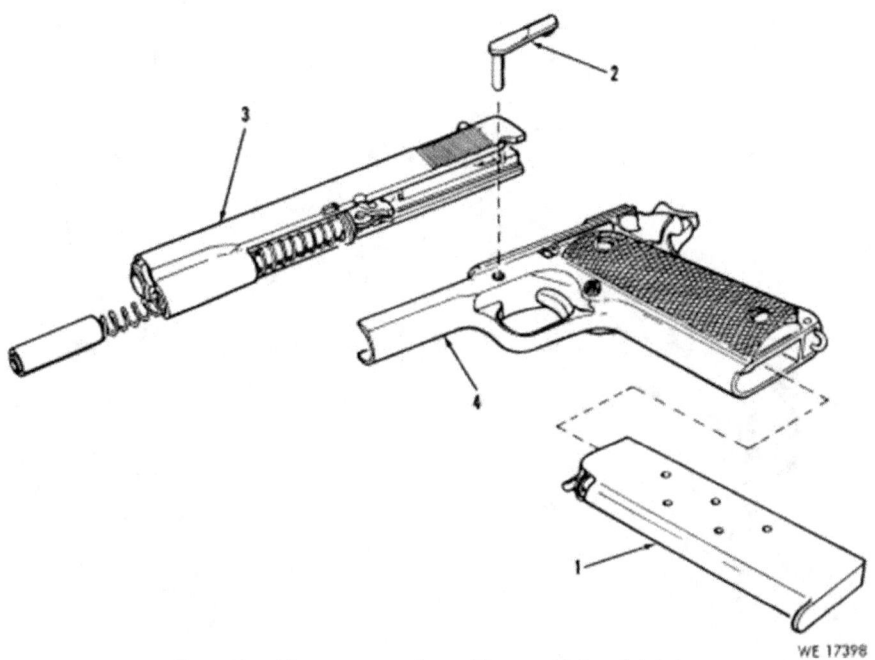

Figure B-1. Major groups and assemblies—partial exploded view

WE 17398

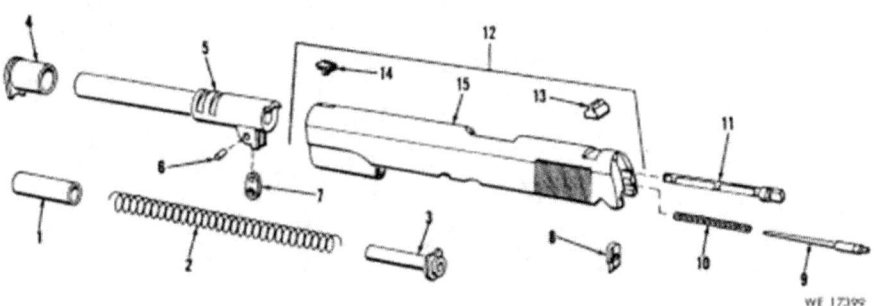

Figure B-2. Slide group — exploded view.

WE 17399

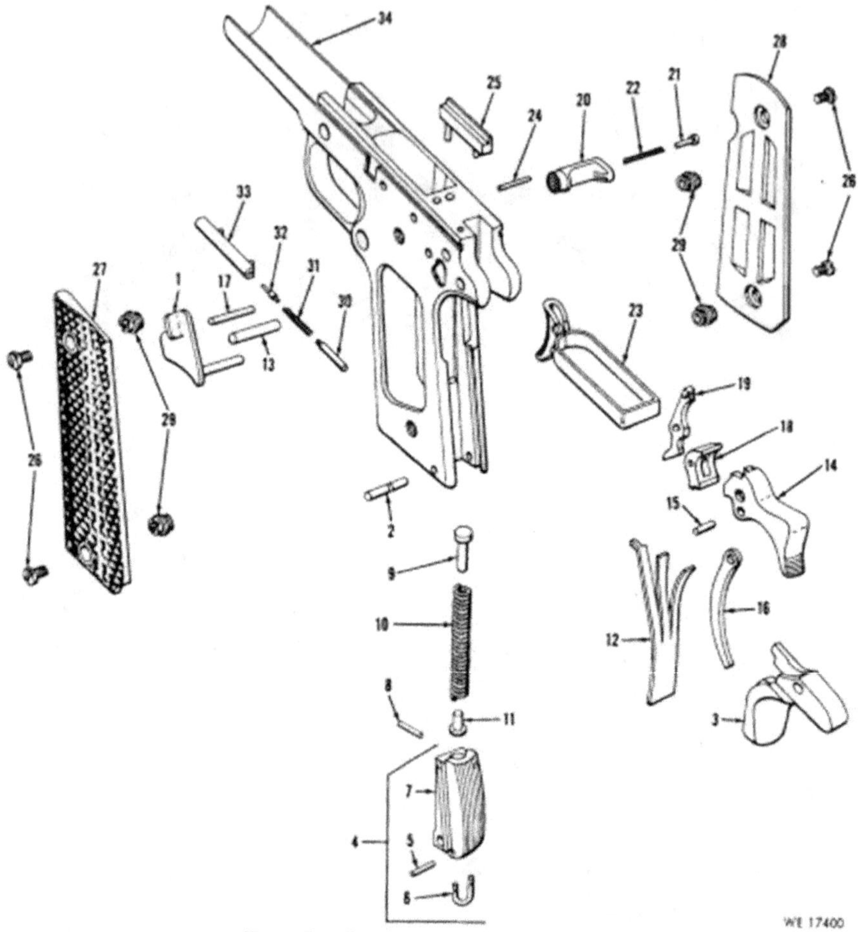

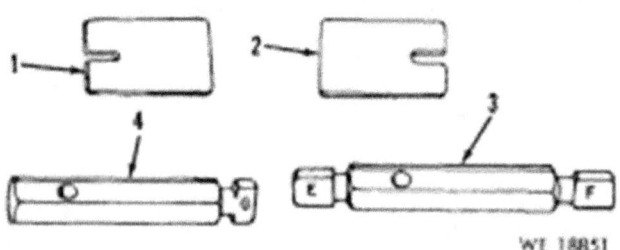

Figure B-3. Receiver group—exploded view.

WE 17400

Figure B-4. ~Tools and equipment

WE 18851

SECTION IV. INDEX-FEDERAL STOCK NUMBER AND REFERENCE NUMBER CROSS-REFERENCE TO FIGURE AND ITEM NUMBER

FSN/Reference number cross-reference has been omitted from this version due to editor's laziness and the fact that civilians cannot order through military channels anyway.

End of TM 9-1005-211-35

DIRECT SUPPORT, GENERAL SUPPORT,
AND DEPOT MAINTENANCE MANUAL
INCLUDING REPAIR PARTS AND
SPECIAL TOOL LISTS

PISTOL, CALIBER .45, AUTOMATIC: M1911A1,
WITH HOLSTER, HIP, W/ E (1005-673-7961) AND PISTOL,
CALIBER
.45, AUTOMATIC: M1911A1,
WITH HOLSTER, SHOULDER, W /E (1005-561-2003)

www.ingramcontent.com/pod-product-compliance
Lightning Source LLC
Chambersburg PA
CBHW060338290526
45793CB00003B/659